Exploring the Solar System

REVISED EDITION

A History with 22 Activities

MARY KAY CARSON

CHICAGO
REVIEW
PRESS

To future explorers

Library of Congress Cataloging-in-Publication Data

Carson, Mary Kay.
    Exploring the solar system for kids : a history with 22 activities/ Mary Kay Carson.—Revised ed.
    p. cm.
    Includes bibliographical references and index.
    ISBN-13: 978-1-55652-715-9
    ISBN-10: 1-55652-715-2
    1. Outer space—Exploration—Juvenile literature. 2. Astronomy —Study and teaching—Activity programs—Juvenile literature. I. Title.
    QB500.262.C37 2006
    523.2—dc22

                                                2005028284

© 2006, 2008 by Mary Kay Carson
Revised edition
Published by Chicago Review Press, Incorporated
814 North Franklin Street
Chicago, Illinois 60610

ISBN-13: 978-1-55652-715-9
ISBN-10: 1-55652-715-2

Printed in Italy
5 4 3 2 1

Cover and interior design: Joan Sommers Design
Interior illustrations: TJ Romero

PHOTO CREDITS

Pages vi, 10 and back cover, 16 courtesy of Tom Uhlman

Pages 3, PIA00157; 45, P288A; 45, PIA02975; 59, PIA04594; 62, PIA01522; 65, PIA02999; 66, PIA03153; 69, PIA00572; 70, PIA00145; 71, PIA00407; 77, PioneerFlyby; 80, PIA04495; 88, PIA01490; 90, P24652B; 93, JPL-28311; 103, PIA01193; 104, PIA00744; 105, PIA00200; 108, PIA01466; 112, PIA03142; 113, PIA04604; 119, PIA04421; 121, Joy_Crisp_040831; 122, PIA06837; 126, PIA05275; 133, PIA02410; 131; 136, PIA04892; 136, PIA05488; 142, PIA00157; 159, PIA00119 courtesy of the National Aeronautics and Space Administration (NASA) Jet Propulsion Laboratory (JPL)

Pages 7, LC-USZ62-21237; 12, LC-USZ62-7923 courtesy of the Library of Congress, Prints & Photographs Division

Pages 18, Goddard-1926; 25, 74-H-1210; 28, Korolev1954; 30, sputnik1; 31, sputnik2; 32, VAN-9; 38, AS11-40-5903; 41, cosmonauts1960; 42, gagarin01; 42, yurigagarin01; 43, S88-31378; 46, 67-H-218; 49, 68-HC-870; 56, voskhod1965; 67, 74-H-856; 90, 72-H-192; 96, STS061-98-050 courtesy of NASA Headquarters

Pages 20, MSFC-8007271; 21, MSFC-9138034; 21, MSFC-9248163; 26, MSFC-9906009; 27, MSFC-9131496; 32, MSFC-5700940; 33, MSFC-5800669; 34, MSFC-5800537; 34, MSFC-0200146; 35, MSFC-0100074; 35, MSFC-5663627; 37, MSFC-5900120; 42, MSFC-9248173; 50, MSFC-0101140; 51, MSFC-6901046; 75, MSFC-8915499; 98, MSFC-8663390; 135, MSFC-9249473; 134, MSFC-0201903; 134, MSFC-0201791 courtesy of NASA Marshall Space Flight Center

Page 24 courtesy of the United States Patent and Trademark Office, U.S. Patent # 1,102,653

Pages 24, G-32-04; 138, 091; 143, GL-2002-001476; 144, GL-2002-002528; 157, GL-2002-001140 courtesy of NASA Goddard Space Flight Center

Pages 30, 113, 132 courtesy of NASA

Page 31 courtesy of Wolfgang Hausmann

Pages 36, 59-008A-01A; 60, 64-0771-01A; 64, 75-050D-01A; 71, 75-075A-01F; 72, 75-083C-06F(P-17686); 72, 75-083C-06F(P-21873); 74, 73-085A-01S; 85, 77-084A-01A; 145, 69-059A-01A; 148, 75-075A-01F courtesy of National Space Science Data Center (NSSDC)

Pages 39, 61C-0189; 40, 84PC-0022; 48, BurntCapsule; 67, KSC-74PC-0303; 101, 89PC-0732; 107, 96PC-1130; 134, KSC-01PP-1087; 134, KSC-69PC-0435; 153, KSC-97PC-0610; 158, KSC-97PC-0558 courtesy of NASA Kennedy Space Center

Pages 46; 65, P-12035A; 92, LSPN-1725 courtesy of NASA and NSSDC

Pages 52, S69-31739; 53, AS11-40-5873; 54 and back cover, AS17-147-22526; 55, AS17-145-22157; 55, S73-15713; 57, AS17-134-20530 courtesy of NASA Johnson Space Center

Page 58 courtesy of Arne Koertzinger

Pages 68, AC76-0564; 78, AC73-9253; 78, 79-H-732; 82, AC77-0850; 89, AC97-0036-1 courtesy of NASA Ames Research Center

Page 72 courtesy of Michael Okoniewski

Pages 76, 94 courtesy of European Space Agency (ESA)

Page 79 courtesy of the Lunar and Planetary Laboratory, University of Arizona

Pages 83, PIA00343; 84, PIA00400; 86, PIA00032; 88, PIA00340; 109; 110, PIA03883; 112, PIA03143; 114; 117, PIA06992; 124, 125; 127; 139, PIA03101; 141, PIA00104; 154, PIA00032; 155, PIA01492; 160, PIA05569 courtesy of NASA/JPL-Caltech

Page 99 courtesy of the Space Telescope Science Institute (STScI), R. Evans, J. Trauger, H. Hammel and the HST Comet Science Team, and NASA

Page 100 courtesy of the Space Telescope Science Institute (STScI) and NASA

Page 116, PIA06425 courtesy of NASA/JPL/GSFC/Ames

Page 117 courtesy of ESA/NASA/University of Arizona

Pages 120, PIA05755; 120, PIA05634; 123, PIA05591 courtesy of NASA/JPL/Cornell

Page 128 courtesy of Johns Hopkins University Applied Physics Laboratory/Southwest Research Institute

Page 130, STSCI-PR94-17/MRPS87787 courtesy of Dr. R. Albrecht, ESA/ESO Space Telescope European Coordinating Facility, and NASA

Page 130, STSCI-PRC96-09A/MRPS87785 courtesy of Alan Stern (Southwest Research Institute), Marc Buie (Lowell Observatory), NASA, and ESA

Page 131 courtesy of NASA, ESA, and G. Bacon (STScI)

Pages 133, 135 courtesy of NASA/Johns Hopkins University Applied Physics Laboratory/Carnegie Institution of Washington

Page 146 courtesy of National Space Science Data Center, NASA Goddard Space Flight Center

Page 154, PIA02963 courtesy of Kenneth Seidelmann, U.S. Naval Observatory, and NASA

Page 156 courtesy of NASA/Southwest Research Institute

Acknowledgments

This book wouldn't have happened without the enthusiasm and support of editor and fellow space buff Jerome Pohlen—thanks, Jerry! Photographer Tom Uhlman deserves many thanks for contributing his always-amazing photographs. Thanks also to the Lunar and Planetary Laboratory at the University of Arizona for graciously supplying the photograph of Gerard Kuiper.

Note to Readers

Today we know a lot about the planets, moons, comets, and asteroids of our solar system. But while humans have walked on the Moon, we've never set foot on any other planet. So how do we know that Mars is covered in rusty dust and that yellow clouds float over Venus? How did we take the temperature of the Sun and figure out what's inside comets? That's what this book is all about. It tells the story of *how* we discovered and learned what we know about our solar system.

Starting on page 137 is a "Field Guide to the Solar System." This reference section features basic facts about the planets and their moons, the Sun, dwarf planets, comets, and asteroids, and time lines detailing our exploration of them.

Astronomers and space scientists are making new discoveries about the solar system all the time. At this moment space missions and astronomical observatories are further exploring the planets, moons, dwarf planets, comets, and asteroids of our solar system. While this book is as up-to-date as possible, new findings emerge every day. The Web sites found on page 164 and within the Exploration Time Lines in the "Field Guide to the Solar System" can update you on future discoveries and help you to continue learning. Keep exploring!

Contents

Time Line

Prehistory Humans mark the passage of time with lunar phases and observe Mercury, Venus, Mars, Jupiter, and Saturn with the naked eye

Ancient Times Chinese, Babylonians, Greeks, and Egyptians record their observations of the night sky

A.D. 140 Ptolemy writes that Earth is the center of the cosmos

1543 Copernicus states that the Sun is the center of the cosmos

1609 Galileo Galilei builds the first astronomical telescope and begins observations

1616 Johannes Kepler publishes his third law of planetary motion

1668 Isaac Newton builds the first reflecting telescope after defining the laws of gravity

1758 Halley's comet appears, just as Edmond Halley had predicted 53 years earlier

1781 William Herschel discovers Uranus

1801 Giuseppe Piazzi discovers Ceres

1846 Johann Galle discovers Neptune

1926 Robert Goddard launches the world's first liquid-fueled rocket

1930 Clyde Tombaugh discovers Pluto

1944 Wernher von Braun's V-2 rockets begin falling on England

1957 World's first satellite, *Sputnik 1*, orbits Earth

1958 NASA is formed and launches its first spacecraft, *Pioneer 1*

1959 *Luna 2* is the first spacecraft to impact the Moon

  Luna 3 returns the first photographs of the Moon's far side

1961 Yuri Gagarin, aboard *Vostok 1*, is the first human in space and in Earth's orbit

1962 *Mariner 2* to Venus is the first successful space probe to another planet

1964 *Ranger 7* is the first space probe to send back close-ups of the Moon

1965 *Mariner 4* is the first spacecraft to successfully fly by Mars

1966 *Luna 9* is the first space probe to "soft land" on the Moon and photogrpah its surface

1967 *Venera 4* to Venus is the first atmospheric space probe

1968 *Zond 5* is the first spacecraft to fly around the Moon and return to Earth

1969 *Apollo 11* delivers the first humans to the Moon

1970 *Venera 7* to Venus is the first spacecraft to successfully land on another planet

Luna 16 is the first sample return mission, bringing soil samples from the Moon's surface back to Earth

Luna 17 delivers the first robotic rover, *Lunokhod 1*, to the Moon

1971 *Mariner 9*, in its journey to Mars, is the first planetary orbiter

1973 *Pioneer 10* is the first spacecraft to pass through the asteroid belt and the first to visit Jupiter

1974 *Mariner 10* is the first spacecraft to use gravity assist and the first to fly by Mercury

1975 *Venera 9* is the first Venus orbiter and the first lander to send photos from the surface of another planet

1976 *Viking 1* and *Viking 2* are the first soft landers on Mars

1977 James Elliot discovers Uranus's rings

1979 *Pioneer 11* is the first space probe to visit Saturn

1983 *Venera 15* is the first radar mapping probe to Venus

1986 *Vega 1, Vega 2, Sakigake, Suisei,* and *Giotto* make flyhys of Halley's comet

Voyager 2 is the first spacecraft to visit Uranus

1990 *Hubble Space Telescope* is the first orbiting telescope

1991 *Galileo* is the first space probe to fly by an asteroid, Gaspra

1994 *Hubble Space Telescope* creates the first maps of Pluto and photographs the comet Shoemaker-Levy 9's impact with Jupiter

1995 *Galileo* is the first spacecraft to orbit Jupiter and releases the first atmospheric probe to Jupiter

1997 Comet Hale-Bopp is visible to the naked eye

Mars Pathfinder delivers the first rover, *Sojourner*, to Mars

2001 *NEAR Shoemaker* to Eros is the first spacecraft to orbit and land on an asteroid

2004 *Cassini* is the first orbiter of Saturn

2005 *Huygens* sets down on Titan, the first probe to land in the outer solar system

Mike Brown discovers Eris

2006 First spacecraft to visit Pluto, *New Horizons*, launches

Prehistory-1900: Spying on the Heavens

The next time you're outside on a clear night, look up. You won't be the first person to marvel at the Moon and stars. Studying the lights in the night sky is something that humans have always done. People have used recognizable star patterns, called constellations, to mark the passing of time for thousands of years. Ancient peoples used star calendars to help time crop plantings and to move to new hunting grounds as the seasons changed.

The night sky's pattern of stars, or starscape, is like a background of lights out in space. Our view of the starscape shifts during the year as the Earth travels around the Sun. The Big Dipper, for example, appears handle up in the sky during the summer and handle down during the winter. But the Big Dipper always keeps its ladle shape because it's not the stars, but Earth, that is moving. This changing view allows us to use the constellations as a kind of calendar.

If you counted all the stars you could see while looking up at the night sky, you'd get to about 3,000 before running out of bright dots. But you would have miscounted by a few. That's because some of the very brightest dots aren't actually stars.

The bright evening star near the Moon isn't a star at all. It's the planet Venus.

The ones that shine without twinkling are really planets. Depending on when you look and how much city light is around, you can see the planets Mercury, Venus, Mars, Jupiter, and Saturn with just your eyes.

WONDERING ABOUT WANDERERS

In ancient times the Chinese, Babylonians, Greeks, and Egyptians recorded their observations of stars. They noticed that five "stars" were different from the thousands of others—they didn't twinkle. They also noted that these brightly shining "stars" seemed to move differently, too. On most nights, these five "wandering stars" travel from east to west. But they show up in different places on the starscape from one night to the next. And their speed and direction change, too. Sometimes they move quickly, but other times slowly—or even stop, then go backward! The odd movements of the "wandering stars" seemed purposeful, or intelligent, to some ancient cultures. Many believed that the wanderers were gods moving back and forth as they went about their heavenly business.

The five "wandering stars" are, of course, not stars at all. They're the planets Mercury, Venus, Mars, Jupiter, and Saturn. They seem to "wander" across the night sky because, unlike stars, planets really do move. Planets don't twinkle like stars because planets are so much closer to us. The strong, steady light of the nearby Sun reflects off a planet's entire lit side, causing it to shine a beam of light toward Earth. By comparison, from Earth faraway stars look like single points of light. Those tiny points of weak starlight get bounced and blurred coming through Earth's atmosphere. That's what causes stars to twinkle.

The nearest planet, Venus, is 67 million miles (108 million km) from Earth. That seems far, but not compared to the nearest star, *Alpha Centauri*. It's 25 trillion miles (40 trillion km) away! That's the difference between walking a single step and hiking across the state of Indiana! These five planets are not a part of the unchanging starscape background. They're part of our solar system.

Everything in the solar system—planets and their moons, dwarf planets, asteroids, and comets—travels around the Sun. But each planet

Why They Wander

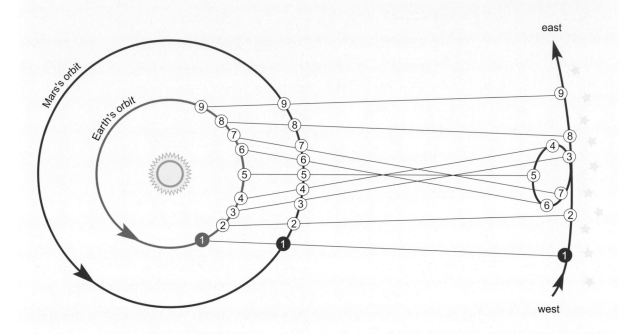

The planets can appear to slow down, stop, and change direction against the background of the unchanging starscape. This is because the closer the planets are to the Sun, the speedier their orbit. This diagram shows how Mars looks like it's moving backward each time the faster-moving Earth passes it up. The looping path on the right shows how Mars's travels look from Earth.

revolves, or orbits, around the Sun at its own uneven pace—all while the Earth is doing the same. Looking at moving planets from a world that is also on the go makes for some odd tricks of perspective. It's like watching a truck as you're passing it on the highway. The truck can look like it's standing still or even slipping backward, but it isn't really. Your car is just moving faster and passing it by (see "Why They Wander," page 2).

Sometime around the sixth century B.C., ancient Greek scholars decided that the five "wandering stars" were not really gods who were out for heavenly strolls. The scholars began to carefully chart the paths of the planets, create tables of measurements, and work on ideas that would explain the planets' movements. They were some of the world's first astronomers.

FINDING THE COSMOS'S CENTER

By the second century, ancient scholars had come up with an explanation of how the planets moved that didn't involve gods. It was hammered out by a Greek astronomer, mathematician, and geographer working in the great Egyptian city of Alexandria. His name was Ptolemy (TALL-uh-me).

Spy the Evening Star activity

There are five planets visible to the naked eye. But Venus is by far the easiest to see. Often called the "Evening Star," Venus is the third-brightest object in Earth's sky, after the Sun and the Moon. Look for Venus around sunrise or sunset, not in the middle of the night. It will appear close to the horizon near the Sun. (Remember, never look directly at the Sun!) When and where Venus appears in the sky depends on where it is in its orbit around the Sun. Check a night-sky calendar in a magazine about astronomy or telescopes, in the weather section of many newspapers, or on a sky calendar Web site (see page 165).

If you have a pair of seven-power (7x) or stronger binoculars you can see Venus change shape over time. You can even track the shapes Venus goes through (called phases) and prove that Venus orbits the Sun—just like Galileo did. Just sketch Venus's shape night after night and see how it changes phases. Hope for clear weather!

This 16th-century engraving illustrates the universe according to Ptolemy. The watery Earth is in the center with the Moon and the Sun circling around it, and the zodiac constellations lay beyond.

According to his theory of the universe, Earth is a sphere that never spins or moves. Instead, it is fixed in the center of the cosmos, and all the other planets and the Sun orbit around it. Ptolemy explained the wandering paths of the planets by claiming that these planets moved around in their own mini-orbits within different layers of celestial stuff. Ptolemy's theory may not sound that convincing today, but it was then. If you accept the Ptolemaic system of circles and spheres as true, the system can be used to predict the paths of the planets across the night sky pretty well. Maybe this explains why the Ptolemaic system was widely accepted in both Europe and the Middle East for more than a thousand years!

It took a Polish clergyman to finally change people's ideas about the center of the cosmos. Nicolaus Copernicus (Coh-PER-nih-cus) was born Mikolaj Kopernik in 1473. After studying law and medicine in Italy, Copernicus took up math and astronomy. Then he moved back to Poland, became a church official, and started studying the night sky. Most astronomers during the 1500s worked on fine-tuning the Ptolemaic system.

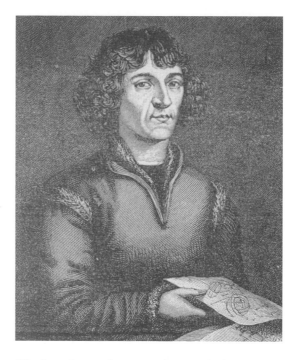

Nicolaus Copernicus put the Sun in its proper place—the center of the solar system.

But Copernicus decided that Ptolemy's system was too ridiculously complicated to be true. He decided that the simplest way to explain how the cosmos moved was to put the Sun in the center, with all of the planets, including Earth, revolving around it. He thought the Earth must spin itself around once every day. Copernicus wrote up his ideas in a book called *On the Revolutions of the Heavenly Spheres*.

It's unlikely that Copernicus knew that his ideas would soon start the age of modern astronomy. But he did know that saying the Sun was the center of the cosmos could get him into trouble. Copernicus was an official of the church, after all. And the church stated that the Earth was the most important thing in the cosmos—that it was unlike any other planet and that it rightfully belonged in the center of the universe. That's why Copernicus put off publishing his book until he was dying. He died in bed after seeing the first copy of it on May 24, 1543.

Copernicus's Sun-centered, or heliocentric, view of the cosmos helped bring about the scientific Renaissance. By 1600 most astronomers accepted that the Sun was the center of the cosmos, that all the planets circled around it, and that the Earth spun around, creating day and night. But Copernicus's theory had a big problem. It didn't actually predict the path of the planets very well. Why didn't Copernicus's cosmic model match what astronomers were seeing in the night sky? It was a question that

pestered Johannes Kepler for many years. Kepler was the German-born assistant of Tycho Brahe (BRA-hey), the greatest observer of the planets at the time (this was before Galileo and the invention of the telescope). For many years Brahe made detailed records of where each planet was in its night-by-night path through the dark sky. After Brahe died, Kepler replaced him as the astronomer at an observatory in Prague.

Kepler knew firsthand that Brahe's observations were absolutely accurate. So why didn't they match Copernicus's theory of how the planets should move across the sky? Kepler decided to study the problem by concentrating on the movement of just one planet—Mars. Kepler had Brahe's detailed records of Mars's movements—and he knew they were right. For six years, with failing eyesight, Kepler tried combinations of circular orbits that would put Mars in the positions that Brahe had observed. Finally, in 1609, Kepler figured out that there was no magic combination of circular orbits. Mars's orbit was not circular. It was oval shaped, or elliptical.

Copernicus's theory had the planets orbiting the Sun in simple circles. But Kepler discovered

Johannes Kepler (1571–1630)

Johannes Kepler learned about, and embraced, Copernicus's heliocentric theory in college. He later taught math and astronomy, and then became an assistant to Tycho Brahe. Kepler's discovery that the planets move in elliptical orbits led to Kepler's laws of planetary motion:

Law 1: All the planets follow an elliptical orbit around the Sun.

Law 2: The planets move faster when they are passing closer to the Sun.

Law 3: Each planet's orbit time is related mathematically to its distance from the Sun. (This means that you can calculate how far away a planet is from the Sun if you know how long it takes the planet to make one orbit around it.)

Kepler wrote the following epitaph for himself: "I used to measure the heavens, now I shall measure the shadows of the earth. Although my soul was from heaven, the shadow of my body lies here."

Outlining Orbits

activity

Johannes Kepler's discovery that the planets move around the Sun in elliptical, not circular, orbits led the way to his laws of planetary motion. Create and compare a circular orbit and an elliptical orbit in this activity.

YOU'LL NEED

8¹⁄₂" x 11" (22-cm x 28-cm) sheet of white paper

Pencil or pen

Piece of cardboard (or an old magazine) that is at least 8¹⁄₂" x 11" (22 cm x 28 cm)

Tape

2 pushpins

5" (13-cm) length of string tied into a loop

Colored pencil or pen

1. Fold paper in half, then fold that half again. Open the paper up and use a pencil or pen to draw a line in the longest horizontal crease.
2. The spot where the unlined crease intersects with the line you drew is the midpoint. Label the midpoint "Sun." Put the paper on the cardboard or old magazine and tape down the corners so it doesn't slide around.
3. Push a pushpin into the Sun midpoint. Place the string loop around the pushpin. Hold the pencil upright inside the loop of string until it's taut. Move the pencil around inside the string loop to make a circle, as shown below. This creates the path of a circular orbit, which no planet has!

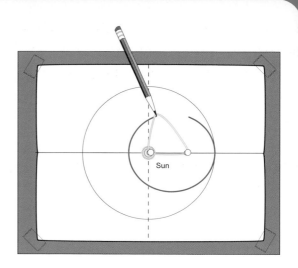

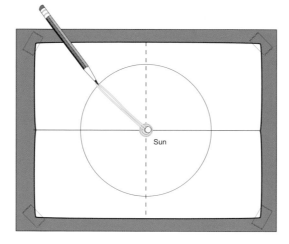

4. Now push the other pushpin somewhere on the horizontal line you drew. It can be either to the left or the right of the Sun; it doesn't matter. Place the string loop around both pushpins. Use the colored pencil or pen to draw an oval inside the string loop, as shown. This path shows an elliptical orbit, which every planet has!

5. Take the pushpins out, remove the string, and compare the two orbits. Notice how a planet traveling on this elliptical path wouldn't always be the same distance from the Sun, like a planet traveling on a circular path would.

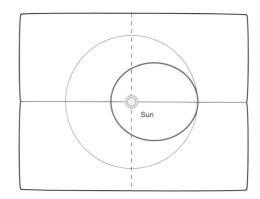

that all the planets have elliptical orbits. Once he made this breakthrough, Kepler solved other mysteries about how and why the planets move as they do. In an elliptical orbit, a planet is sometimes nearer to the Sun than it is at other times. Kepler discovered that a planet's movement speeds up when it's closer to the Sun. He also discovered that the longer it took a planet to orbit the Sun, the farther away it was from the Sun. These ideas about how planets move became known as Kepler's laws (see the Kepler biography on page 5). Kepler's laws backed up Copernicus's theory of a Sun-centered cosmos. But it would take a colleague of Kepler's to actually prove it to the world.

SEEING NEW WORLDS IN A NEW WAY

In the spring of 1609, an Italian scientist heard about a new instrument that showed faraway things as though they were nearby. Remarkable! At 45 years of age, Galileo Galilei set out to build such an instrument himself. Within months Galileo had built a device that magnified objects to twenty times their size. By the fall of 1609

Galileo was doing what no one had ever done before. He was observing the heavens with a telescope.

What Galileo saw through his telescope proved that Copernicus and Kepler were right. When Galileo observed Venus through a telescope, he saw that it went through phases—just like the Moon does. This proved that Venus orbits the Sun, just like the Moon orbits the Earth. Galileo also discovered that the Moon wasn't smooth, like everyone thought. He could see craters and mountains on the Moon with his telescope. Galileo also saw four never-before-seen moons circling Jupiter. And he spotted something odd near the edges of Saturn. (It would later turn out to be the planet's rings.)

Galileo's discoveries changed everything. They not only provided the proof needed to forever push Earth out of the center of the cosmos, but the discoveries also showed that the Moon and the planets weren't godlike points of light, made of celestial material and beyond the understanding of humble humans. These were real places—actual worlds with rocks, mountains, and moons of their own. Earth

Galileo Galilei (1564–1642)

Galileo Galilei studied medicine as a young man, but soon started making scientific discoveries. Galileo became the first true modern scientist, showing that careful experiments and observations could explain how nature worked. Galileo helped disprove much of medieval science. His ideas were an important part of the Renaissance. Galileo discovered new laws of falling bodies and demonstrated the laws of equilibrium. He also contributed the principles of flotation and inertia.

After writing *Dialogue Concerning the Two Chief Systems of the World*, Galileo was arrested for having "held and taught" Copernican doctrine, which the Roman Catholic Church considered heresy. He lived under house arrest for the rest of his life. Galileo became blind—some say from looking at the Sun. The Pope exonerated Galileo 350 years after his death.

Sir Isaac Newton and his small, but revolutionary, reflecting telescope.

wasn't the unique center of the cosmos. It was simply one of many worlds that orbited the Sun. Earth was in the Sun's realm. Our world belonged to a solar system.

REASON BEHIND MOTION

When the plague hit Cambridge, England, in 1665, Isaac Newton decided to leave town. While waiting for the outbreak to pass at his family's country home, an apple caught Newton's eye. He watched as the fruit fell from its tree to the earth below. It got him thinking. Could the force that pulled the apple to the ground be the same force that makes the Earth orbit around the Sun? It is the same force. Newton had discovered gravity.

Gravity is the force of attraction among all matter. How the gravitational attraction of one thing affects another depends on mass and distance. Objects that are far apart have less gravitational attraction to each other than objects that are close together. And more massive objects create a greater gravitational force of attraction than smaller ones do.

Newton published these ideas in his 1687 book *Principia Mathematica*. In it both Kepler's laws of planetary motion and Galileo's observations are explained by one simple law of universal gravitation. The puzzle of why and how the planets moved was now solved. Astronomers left the mystery of planetary movements behind. It was time to begin exploring the nature of the planets themselves—up close.

ZOOMING IN ON THE HEAVENS

Discovering how gravity holds the universe together wasn't Isaac Newton's only contribution to astronomy. He also created a better telescope. Galileo's biggest telescope was a metal tube less

Optical Telescopes

The light reaching Earth from faraway planets and distant stars is very faint. The job of a telescope is to collect as much of that faint light as possible, focus that light, and allow the viewer to see where it came from. Like the human eye, optical telescopes work by collecting visible light. They magnify distant objects by focusing that collected light. Astronomers use three basic types of optical telescopes to look at planets and stars.

The first telescopes, including those of Galileo's and Kepler's, were **refracting telescopes**. This type of telescope uses a combination of lenses to bend, or refract, the light entering the telescope tube. The telescope's large convex objective lens collects the light coming from the Moon or a star and refracts it so that it's concentrated at a point near the back of the tube. That point is called the focus. The eyepiece lens magnifies the image created at the focus point and brings it to the eye.

Reflecting telescopes, like the kind Isaac Newton built, use curved mirrors to collect the light entering the telescope. Light from the Moon or a star is reflected off a large concave primary mirror at the far end of the telescope tube. The curve in the mirror concentrates the reflected light onto a secondary mirror. This small mirror reflects the light toward the eyepiece lens.

Modern telescopes often use combinations of reflecting mirrors and refracting lenses to collect and focus light. These so-called **compound telescopes** have wide fields of view and sharp images. The light entering the compound telescope passes through a refracting lens on its way to a primary mirror at the back of the tube. The large primary mirror collects the incoming light and reflects it to a curved mirror. This small mirror concentrates the light into a focus and passes it through a hole in the primary mirror to the eyepiece.

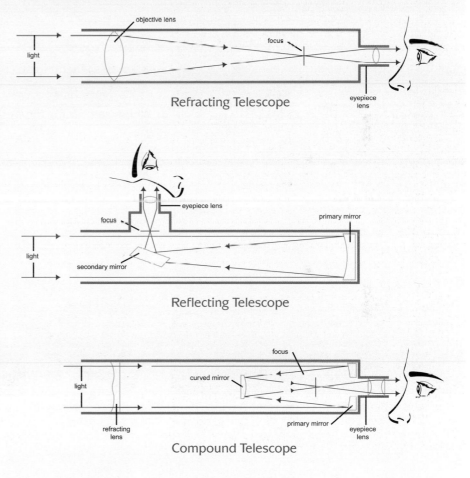

Refracting Telescope

Reflecting Telescope

Compound Telescope

Using telescopes and binoculars to observe planets and stars is a fun way to learn astronomy.

than two inches (5 cm) wide and about three feet (1 m) long. Inside the tube were two lenses, one at each end. The lens that Galileo looked through is called the eyepiece lens. It was concave, or curved inward like a bowl. The lens at the far end is called the objective lens. It was convex, or curved outward. This combination of lenses zoomed in so well that Galileo could only look at a fourth of the Moon at a time! The telescope had what's called a very small field of view. Johannes Kepler improved on Galileo's telescope design by using a concave lens for both the objective and eyepiece lenses. This produced an upside-down image, but the field of view was larger. Kepler could see the whole Moon at once with his telescope.

Another problem of early telescopes like Kepler's and Galileo's was that the edges of the crude lenses acted like prisms. This caused a rainbow halo to appear around the image. During the 1660s Isaac Newton discovered that sunlight is actually made up of many colors of light. While studying light, Newton figured out that if he replaced his telescope's lenses with curved mirrors, the rainbow halo vanished. Newton had built the first reflecting telescope. Newton's first reflecting telescope was only six inches (15 cm) long, and its primary mirror was just an inch (2.5 cm) wide. But the telescope was so powerful that he could see Jupiter's moons with it!

The power of a telescope depends on how much light it can collect. The more light collected, the brighter the image and the greater the detail seen. In general, the larger a telescope's light-gathering lens or mirror, the better the view. It takes a very large telescope to collect light from a very distant star!

At first, astronomers used telescopes to get a closer look at what they already knew was out there. They zoomed in on the Moon, charted Venus's phases, and spotted Saturn's rings. They also used their new telescopic views to help calculate the planets' sizes, distances from the Sun, and rotation periods. To do this, astronomers would pick out visual markers on Jupiter, for instance, and watch through a telescope as the planet spun around. Then they'd keep track of the amount of time that passed until the same markers came back around. That amount of time was Jupiter's rotation period, or day length.

Build a Telescope activity

When Galileo Galilei set out to build his first telescope, he used two tubes, one that fit inside the other, and lenses from spectacles. You can make a similar simple refracting telescope in this activity.

YOU'LL NEED

38-mm-diameter, 300-mm–focal-length double convex lens*

Cardboard paper towel tube

Clear packing tape

5" x 9" (13-cm x 23-cm) piece of dark-colored poster board (or other heavy paper)

38-mm-diameter, 200-mm–focal-length double convex lens*

* You can buy these common lenses at scientific or teaching supply stores.

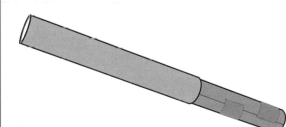

1. Place the 300-mm-focal-length lens inside one end of the paper towel tube so that it's even with the end of the tube. This is the objective lens.
2. Tape the lens in place. Try to get tape on only the outer edge of the lens.
3. Roll the piece of poster board into a tube shape and slide it into the paper towel tube.
4. Slide the poster board tube in and out of the paper towel tube to figure out how tightly rolled it needs to be. It should slide easily, but be tight enough to hold its place without slipping down. When you've determined the correct size, tape the poster board into a permanent tube.
5. Place the 200-mm-focal-length lens into one end of the poster board tube. Line up the lens with the end of the tube and tape it to the tube. Try to get tape on only the outer edges of the lens. This is your eyepiece lens.
7. Place the open end of the poster board tube into the open end of the paper towel tube. Your telescope is finished!
8. Look through the eyepiece lens at a distant object. Yes, it will be upside down! To focus on the object, slide the poster board tube in and out of the paper towel tube until the image is clear.

This 40-foot-long (12-m-long) reflecting telescope was one of William Herschel's giants. The largest Herschel telescope had a mirror four feet (1.2 m) in diameter.

Like celestial surveyors, astronomers could use their new telescopes to estimate how far away the planets are, too. Giovanni Cassini (see page 116) set out to do just that in 1672, during the time when Mars's orbit brought the planet closest to Earth. The plan was for Cassini to stay in Paris while a fellow astronomer went to French Guiana, thousands of miles away in South America. From their two distant viewpoints, each astronomer observed Mars in relation to the background starscape. Once reunited, the men measured how far apart their two views of Mars appeared in relation to the starscape. This phenomenon, in which objects appear to be in different locations when viewed from different places, is called parallax. Knowing the Mars parallax and the distance from Paris to French Guiana, the rest was simple geometry. Cassini calculated that Mars was about 41 million miles (66 million km) away. He wasn't off by much, only about 7 percent over.

As telescopes got bigger and better, astronomers started looking at more than the familiar. They began investigating brand new things and places never before glimpsed—including entire new worlds.

A WHOLE NEW WORLD

William Herschel didn't plan on becoming a scientist. Like his father, he was a musician. But after reading a book about how telescopes work, Herschel decided to try one for himself. The former organist quickly grew bored with looking at what everyone else could see in the night sky. He wanted to see farther than anyone had before. Hershel knew he needed to build the biggest telescope yet to collect such faraway light. So he taught himself to grind his own mirrors, and he fashioned custom eyepieces with magnifying powers of more than 6,000 times. While scanning the sky in 1781 with the first reflecting telescope he'd built, Herschel came across an unusual shining object that didn't look like a star. Herschel tracked the path of what he thought might be a comet over a number of nights. It moved like something within our solar system. It turned out to be a new planet. The planet, named Uranus, was the first planet to be discovered in all of recorded human history.

Once Herschel had discovered a seventh planet in the solar system, astronomers suspected

William Herschel (1738-1822)

William Herschel.

Friedrich Wilhelm Herschel was born in Germany, but moved to England at age 21. Herschel didn't get interested in astronomy until middle age. His younger sister Caroline studied astronomy with him and became his lifelong assistant and an important astronomer herself. Caroline Herschel discovered eight comets and three new nebulae.

William Herschel discovered Uranus and two of its moons, two moons of Saturn, and more than 2,500 stars. His studies and discoveries proved that gravity governed not only our solar system, but also the stars beyond it. Herschel's observations of faraway stars in all directions gave rise to the revolutionary idea that our own solar system was part of a galaxy. Herschel was knighted in 1816.

Caroline Herschel.

This early photograph of the Moon was taken at the Paris Observatory in 1900.

there might be others, too. This was especially true after astronomers did some math. The clue was that Uranus's predicted path around the Sun didn't match what astronomers saw through the telescope. What if the gravitational force of some unknown planet was tugging Uranus off its predicted path as it orbited the Sun?

In 1843 a young English mathematician named John C. Adams set out to calculate just where an eighth planet might be. Adams did the math and figured out that an eighth planet about 1 billion miles (1.6 billion km) past Uranus would be in the right place to explain Uranus's observed orbital path. Adams sent his calculations to the Astronomer Royal of England, who unfortunately ignored them. Meanwhile, a young French mathematician named Urbain J. J. Leverrier soon calculated the same position for an eighth planet. Leverrier had better luck than Adams when he sent his predictions to the astronomer Johann Galle. Galle had just finished charting the stars where the planet was believed to be. On September 23, 1846, Galle found an eighth planet. It was named Neptune.

NEW TOOLS FOR A NEW CENTURY

Neptune might have been found sooner if astronomers had been able to use a newfangled invention in their search—photography. Think for a moment what astronomy was like before photography. Imagine having to draw star charts or maps by hand as you looked through a telescope. If you later wanted to verify that something you'd drawn was in fact correct, you had to wait until the next clear night of telescope viewing. Photography changed all that when astronomers starting snapping photos in the second half of the 1800s. Being able to take photographs through a telescope and study them later made looking for distant objects in crowded starscapes much easier. It also created a permanent record—scientific proof—of what was seen.

Astronomer David Gill borrowed a camera in 1882 to photograph a comet through a telescope in South Africa. But Gill got much more than just a snapshot of the comet. When the photograph was developed, all kinds of never-before-noticed stars showed up in the picture's background. What Gill and other astronomers like him had discovered was the power of photographic film to collect light—more light than the human eye was able to. Objects too faint for astronomers to see through a telescope will show up in photographs. This made photography more than just a recording device. Photography became an important tool for astronomy.

Another new invention became a powerful tool for learning about the solar system in the late 1800s. A spectroscope is a device that magnifies and splits visible light into bands of color called spectral lines. It's like a telescope and a prism combined. A spectroscope collects the light entering a telescope, splits it with a prism, and displays an image of the spectral lines so they can be measured. The patterns of spectral lines coming from a planet or star can tell an astronomer a lot about it. Each element in the universe—such as iron, sodium, and hydrogen, to name a few—creates its own identifiable spectral line. The spectral lines that come from a planet can tell an astronomer what chemicals are present in that planet's atmosphere or surface.

One of earliest discoveries made with a spectroscope was by an English astronomer named Norman Lockyer. In 1869 Lockyer attached a spectroscope to a 6 inch (15-cm) telescope and used it to observe gas streaming away from the Sun. What Lockyer found was a mystery. The solar spectral lines didn't match any element that people knew of at the time. Lockyer had discovered helium!

Astronomers (today they'd be called astrophysicists) soon turned spectroscopes toward other stars, as well as toward the planets. In 1905 Jupiter's spectral lines showed gases that would later be identified as ammonia and methane. And in 1909 an astronomer at the famous Lick Observatory in California used spectral lines coming from Mars to correctly conclude that there was no water in its atmosphere.

Early spectroscopes were attached to telescopes. The round disk near the astronomer's hand is a rotating plate of different light-splitting prisms.

Modern observatories, like Kitt Peak National Observatory in Arizona, have telescopes and astronomical instruments that measure and look for all types of electromagnetic radiation.

Spectroscopy proved what astronomers had been seeing in their telescopes—that the planets, moons, and the Sun are made of the same elements that make up the Earth. Everything in the solar system is made of the same stuff.

Of course, the visible light that is split and measured in a spectroscope is only one of the many types of electromagnetic radiation found in the universe. And it would turn out that tools that could measure other types of electromagnetic radiation—such as radio waves, infrared light, x-rays, and gamma rays—would also provide researchers valuable information about the solar system. But those discoveries would have to wait for a new century to mature a bit. The upcoming 20th century had quite a lot in store for astronomers. Humans would find out more about their solar system than they had in all previous centuries combined. And we'd be traveling there as well.

CD Spectroscope — activity

A spectroscope splits visible light into bands of color, called spectral lines, that are distinct for different kinds of light and chemical elements. Early spectroscopes used prisms to split light. Modern spectroscopes split light using a plate or a mirror that is engraved with tiny parallel grooves or lines, called a diffraction grating. Fortunately, the pitted surface of a used compact disc does the same thing, so you can build a simple spectroscope.

Adult supervision required

YOU'LL NEED

Scissors

9" x 13" (23-cm x 33-cm) piece of poster board or other heavy paper

Ruler

4" (10-cm) diameter dark plastic lid, such as a coffee-can lid

Packing tape

Unwanted, used compact disc

Utility knife, craft knife, or one-edged razor blade

Strong lamp

1. Cut a notch out of the middle of one of the long sides of the piece of poster board, as shown. The notch should be 1¼ inches (3 cm) high and ¼ inch (6 mm) long.

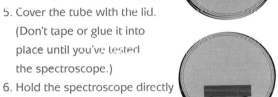

2. Roll the piece of poster board into a fat tube. The can lid will go on top of this tube, so check that the tube is the right width before taping it closed. You can check by setting the unnotched end of the rolled up tube into the upturned can lid, as shown. Tape the tube closed.

3. Set the tube notched side up. Set the compact disc on top of the tube so that the side of the disc that has writing or a printed label is up, facing away from the tube, and the shiny (diffraction grating) side is down, facing into the tube. The compact disc will be a bit bigger than the tube. Tape the disc to the tube, making sure that the notch keeps its rectangular shape.

4. Ask an adult to help you use the knife or razor blade to cut a very thin, 1½-inch-long (3.5-cm-long) slit in the can lid. The slit must be about ¹⁄₁₆ inch (1.5 mm) wide—no more! Make the slit, as shown, so that it will be perpendicular to the notch in the tube.

If you made the slit too wide or too crooked, you can fix it with some electrical tape or even taped-on strips of paper.

5. Cover the tube with the lid. (Don't tape or glue it into place until you've tested the spectroscope.)

6. Hold the spectroscope directly under a strong lamp to test it. The light needs to directly enter the spectroscope through the thin slit in the lid. Watch the compact disc through the notch as you tilt the spectroscope back and forth until you see a thin rainbow on the disc. If you don't see a rainbow, adjust the lid and keep tilting. Once you see the rainbow on the disc, tape or glue the lid in place. It's done!

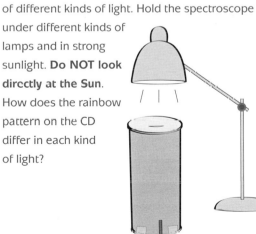

7. Now use the spectroscope to observe the spectra of different kinds of light. Hold the spectroscope under different kinds of lamps and in strong sunlight. **Do NOT look directly at the Sun**. How does the rainbow pattern on the CD differ in each kind of light?

Robert Goddard gets ready to launch the world's first liquid-fueled rocket in 1926.

2 1900-1950s: Rocketing to Space

The solar system seen through 19th-century telescopes looked amazing and strange—yet familiar, too. The planets and Moon no longer appeared to belong to another realm made of celestial stuff, as ancient peoples had assumed. They were actual places. And science was proving that those worlds were bound by the same laws of gravity and made up of the same elements as our own Earth. People began to wonder: will we visit these other worlds someday? Is it possible to travel beyond the Earth?

Writers soon began creating tales about visiting other worlds in a new type, or genre, of fiction called science fiction. Jules Verne wrote books in the late 1800s about traveling to the Moon, and H. G. Wells's *The War of the Worlds* described the invasion of Earth by unfriendly Martians. The fast pace of change as the 19th century turned to the 20th fueled science fiction and dreams of voyaging beyond Earth. People who had grown up riding horses, cooking with wood stoves, and pumping water from wells now had automobiles, electric lights, water faucets, indoor toilets, and telephones. There were even rumors that two brothers from Ohio had

invented a flying machine! Perhaps something like it would one day zoom to the Moon.

The Wright brothers' invention of the airplane was one of two amazing events in 1903 that pushed humanity toward space. The second was an article, published in a Russian science magazine, titled "Exploration of Space by Rocket Devices." Its author was a schoolteacher named Konstantin Tsiolkovsky.

ROCKETS FROM IDEA TO PAPER

Growing up was not easy for Konstantin Tsiolkovsky. His struggling family lived in a small Russian village. When Tsiolkovsky was nine, he caught scarlet fever. The disease left the boy nearly deaf and too sick to go to school. A few years later Tsiolkovsky's mother died. Tsiolkovsky was left at home by himself to study as best he could. Books quickly became both his teachers and his friends. Among those Tsiolkovsky read were the works of Frenchman Jules Verne. Verne's early science fiction works such as *From the Earth to the Moon* started Tsiolkovsky thinking about space travel. At 16 he moved to Moscow to study science. He used an ear trumpet to help him

The Chinese used rocket weapons against the Mongols during the siege of Kai Fung Foo in 1232. The rockets were arrows with tubes of lit gunpowder.

hear the lectures on astronomy, mathematics, and chemistry. After landing a teaching job in a small town, Tsiolkovsky started working hard on his lifetime quest. He began to try to figure out how humans could leave Earth.

"For a long time I thought of the rocket as everyone else did—just as a means of diversion and of petty everyday use," wrote Tsiolkovsky.

Rockets had been around for hundreds of years, after all. The Chinese used rockets in fireworks, and gunpowder-filled rockets were fired against their Mongol enemies as early as 1232. British ships fired rockets against the United States during the War of 1812 in the battle of Fort McHenry. Watching the "rockets' red glare" of that night inspired Francis Scott Key to write about them in a poem that later became the U.S. national anthem, "The Star-Spangled Banner." By Tsiolkovsky's day, rockets were also used as signaling devices on ships, and to shoot lifelines to passengers on sinking ships.

But Tsiolkovsky had a different idea about what rockets might be used for. In order for something to reach space from Earth, it must first escape the strong pull of Earth's gravity. Tsiolkovsky knew that this would take an incredible amount of power. He also understood that once in space, the thing would need a way to keep moving so that it wouldn't get caught in an Earth orbit and become a "satellite." And for that you'd need an engine that could work in a vacuum—there's no air in space. Rockets were the answer, decided Tsiolkovsky. "I do not remember what prompted me to make calculations of [the rocket's] motions. Probably the first seeds of the idea were sown by that great, fantastic author Jules Verne—he directed my thought along certain channels, then came the desire, and after, the work of the mind."

Tsiolkovsky wrote up his ideas on how rockets could be used in space in his 1903 article "Exploration of Space by Rocket Devices." Tsiolkovsky never actually built these rockets. But his ideas and insights laid the groundwork for traveling to space. In a letter to an engineer in 1911, Tsiolkovsky wrote, "Mankind will not remain on the Earth forever, but in the pursuit of light and space, we will, timidly at first, overcome the limits of the atmosphere and then conquer all the area around the Sun."

ROCKETS FROM LAB TO SKY

Tsiolkovsky's work is famous today. But it was unknown in the United States during the early 1900s. Coincidentally, America's leader in rocket development had a lot in common with the Russian theorist he never knew.

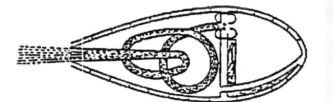

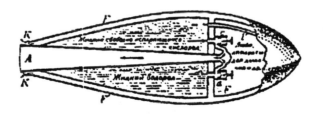

These rocket designs by Konstantin Tsiolkovsky were never built, but they inspired the next generation of rocket scientists.

Konstantin Tsiolkovsky
(1857–1935)

Konstantin Tsiolkovsky started his 40-year teaching career as a math instructor at age 21. While teaching, he experimented and developed his theories about flight, rockets, and space travel. By 1900 Tsiolkovsky had published designs for a metal blimp, an airplane, and a spaceship that used liquid fuel. During the 1920s, he worked on figuring out how multiple-stage rockets could be used in space travel.

Tsiolkovsky's book *On the Moon* was published in 1935, the year he died. It describes the kinds of rockets and space vehicles that Tsiolkovsky thought would be needed to someday visit Earth's moon. Tsiolkovsky didn't live to see rockets reach space or humans landing on the Moon. But his daring ideas and work were forever honored when one of the Moon's newly discovered craters was named after him in the 1960s. Crater Tsiolkovsky is on the side of the Moon that is never seen from Earth. Only rocket-powered spacecraft can reach it.

Rocket Science

Rockets are powered by the reaction principle. Have you ever heard the scientific law that "for every action there is an equal and opposite reaction"? This is Newton's third law of motion, and it's the secret to rocket power.

Think about a balloon you've blown up with air, but haven't tied shut. Now imagine letting go of the balloon. Why does the balloon fly off? The force of the air coming out of the balloon's hole pushes the balloon in the opposite direction. That's action and reaction. In 1883 Tsiolkovsky did the same thing when he opened a cask filled with compressed gas. He also discovered that if he let the same amount of gas out of the cask slowly, the cask moved less. Less action equals less reaction.

Rockets put the reaction principle to maximum use by creating lots of high-pressure gas that can escape in only one way. When gas comes streaming out of a rocket's tail or nozzle, it pushes the rocket in the opposite direction—up. This is how even simple bottle rockets work. Lighting the bottle rocket burns fuel that produces gases. These gases build up inside the bottle rocket and can escape only through the bottom of the rocket. As the gases escape, the rocket is pushed up into the air.

The reaction principle powers all kinds of moving things. Jet engines are also propelled forward by the release of a high-pressure stream of gas in the opposite direction. But jet engines need something that rockets do not—air. Jet engine fuel can't burn without the oxygen in air. A rocket, on the other hand, carries its own source of oxygen, called an oxidizer, along with its fuel. This means that a rocket can go where there is no air—the vacuum of space.

Robert Goddard was also a sickly child. He, too, was inspired by reading early science fiction by Jules Verne and H. G. Wells as a youth. One day, when Goddard was 17, he climbed up an old cherry tree to prune its branches. It was a beautiful, quiet New England autumn afternoon, and young Goddard was soon daydreaming in his perch. "[A]s I looked towards the fields at the east, I imagined how wonderful it would be to make some device which had even the possibility of ascending to Mars, and how it would look on a small scale, if sent up from the meadow at my feet," Goddard later wrote. "I was a different boy when I descended the tree from when I ascended, for existence at last seemed very purposive."

Goddard soon put his new sense of meaning in life to work. As a college student, he experimented with a rocket powered by gunpowder. The clouds of smoke coming from the basement of the physics building got the undivided attention of his professors! By 1914 Goddard had patents for two rocket designs—one that used liquid fuel and another that used multiple stages. A multiple-stage, or multi-stage, rocket

Blast Off a Rocket

activity

Rocket science is about testing designs and making improvements. In this activity you'll first test a rocket engine, then build a rocket to go with it.

YOU'LL NEED

Safety goggles

1 cup water

Plastic 35-mm film canister (the kind with a lid that fits inside the canister's rim)

2–4 effervescing antacid tablets (such as Alka-Seltzer), broken in half

8½" x 11" (22-cm x 28-cm) sheet of paper

Packing tape

Pencil or pen

Poster board (or other heavy paper)

Scissors

1. First, test your rocket engine. Go someplace wide open, like a parking lot, driveway, playground, or gymnasium. Put on your safety goggles to protect your eyes.
2. Pour water into the film canister until it's about one-third full.
3. Drop in one of the effervescing tablet halves and very quickly snap the lid onto the film canister. Set the canister upside down on the ground, and stand back.
4. Watch the rocket engine blast off. Try to remember how high it went relative to a wall, tree, or house. Repeat steps 1–3 until you have a good idea of how high your rocket engine goes. Notice whether it goes straight up or takes a curve, and whether or not it always lands in the same spot.
5. Build a rocket body for your engine. Remove the lid from the film canister. Set the open end of the film canister about ½ inch (1 cm) from the short edge of the sheet of paper. Tape the paper's longer edge to the film canister, as shown.
6. Roll the film canister inside the paper to make a tube and tape it closed.

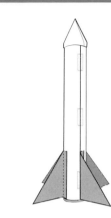

7. Use the poster board to make fins and a nose cone. You can design your own, or you can enlarge the patterns below (set a copy machine to enlarge by 225 percent and trace them). You'll need one nose cone and four fins. Cut out your designs and tape them onto the rocket.
8. Now follow steps 1–4 to load and launch your rocket! Does it fly higher or straighter than the engine alone did? How could you improve the design to make your rocket fly even higher or straighter?

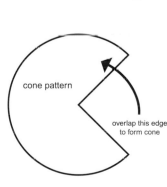

cone pattern

overlap this edge to form cone

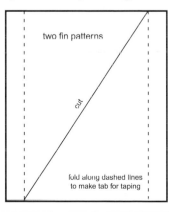

two fin patterns

cut

fold along dashed lines to make tab for taping

Robert Goddard (1882–1945)

Robert Hutchings Goddard began experimenting with rockets while studying physics and continued after becoming a professor.

In 1920, his paper, "A Method for Reaching Extreme Altitudes" was published by the Smithsonian Institution. It was mainly about using rockets to do upper atmosphere weather research. But Goddard ended the paper by suggesting that humans might travel in space. Goddard's suggestion that we might travel to the Moon someday was made fun of in the newspapers. But he told a reporter, "Every vision is a joke until the first man accomplishes it; once realized, it becomes commonplace."

When Robert Goddard died he held 214 patents in rocketry, but he wasn't famous. It wasn't until American rocket scientists began to work on building spacecraft a dozen years later that Goddard's lifetime of work was finally appreciated. Today he is considered the father of modern rocketry. NASA's Goddard Space Flight Center in Greenbelt, Maryland, was named in his honor in 1959.

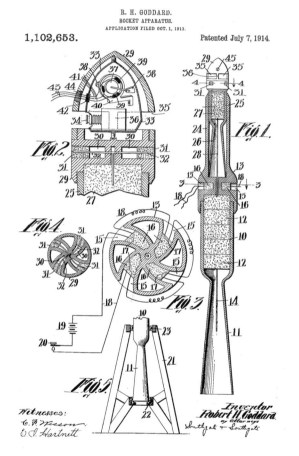

This diagram was part of a patent application for one of Robert Goddard's rocket designs. The patent was granted in 1914.

is made up of smaller rockets stacked on top of larger ones to increase its overall lifting ability. During this time many believed that rockets couldn't work in space because there was no air to push against to get forward motion. But Goddard proved that Newton's reaction principle (see "Rocket Science" sidebar on page 22) worked in the vacuum of space. He fired a pistol inside an airless vacuum chamber and the pistol jerked backward, just like it normally does when fired in the open air. In fact, a rocket gets more thrust in space than on Earth. Where there's no air, there's no air friction to slow it down.

In 1926 Goddard was ready to put all of his theories and ideas to the test. He built the first liquid-fueled rocket. It was small, and it didn't look very powerful (see page 18). But it used quite complex technology. The rocket's fuel was gasoline, and its oxidizer was oxygen cooled to its liquid form. Both ingredients had to be pumped into a combustion chamber, where they burned and produced gas. The rocket's engine was mounted on top of the fuel tank. A metal cone was attached to the tank to protect it from the flame of the rocket's engine.

Robert Goddard tows a rocket through the New Mexico desert around 1930.

On March 16, 1926, Goddard took his rocket out to a nearby farm in Auburn, Massachusetts. He set up his 10-foot-tall (3-m-tall) rocket in the snow, turned on the valves that fed it liquid oxygen, and lit it with a blowtorch. It took about 20 seconds of burning before the rocket had enough thrust to leave the ground. Then it took off, rose to 41 feet (12.5 m), leveled off, and came back down—all within 2½ seconds. The world's first liquid-fueled rocket only flew 184 feet (56 m) and reached a speed of about 60 miles (97 km) per hour. It wasn't a long flight, and Goddard wasn't very happy with the rocket's stability. But history had been made. He described the flight in his diary this way: "It looked almost magical as it rose, without any appreciably greater noise or flame, as if it said, 'I've been here long enough; I think I'll be going somewhere else, if you don't mind.'"

Three years later Goddard loaded some weather equipment onto an improved rocket

A Ninth Planet?

While Goddard was rocketing toward space, scientists continued to explore the solar system the old-fashioned way—with telescopes. In 1905 an astronomer named Percival Lowell (1855–1916) noticed that the gravity of some unknown object seemed to be pulling at the orbits of Neptune and Uranus. He believed the cause was a ninth planet. Lowell spent the last years of his life unsuccessfully searching for it at his observatory in Arizona. In 1929 the Lowell Observatory hired a young amateur astronomer named Clyde W. Tombaugh to take up the search. By examining photos taken with a new astronomical camera, Tombaugh found a "wandering star" that changed position in the constellation Gemini—a ninth planet. The cold, icy world was named Pluto after the Roman god of the dead.

As scientists later learned more about Pluto, they began to doubt whether it was a true planet. Pluto isn't a gas giant like the other outer planets, nor is it like an inner terrestrial planet. Once new worlds out past Pluto started being discovered in the early 21st century, scientists realized that Pluto has more in common with them than with the other eight known planets. In 2006 (see sidebar on page 127) Pluto was reclassified from a planet into a new group of space objects called dwarf planets.

Wernher von Braun
(1912–1977)

Fireworks got Wernher von Braun interested in rockets as a boy in Germany. At age 12 he strapped six rockets to a small wagon and sent it on a wild ride that ended in a big bang. His mother encouraged her son's interest in astronomy by giving him a small telescope. Von Braun became a U.S. citizen in 1955. In a *Time* magazine interview about space flight that was conducted after the 1957 launch of *Sputnik 1* and *Sputnik 2*, von Braun said, "Don't tell me that man doesn't belong out there. Man belongs wherever he wants to go—and he'll do plenty well when he gets there."

Von Braun's team engineered the four-stage rocket, called the Jupiter, which launched *Explorer 1*, the United States's first satellite of Earth. Their Redstone rocket launched Alan Shepard into space in 1961. Most amazing of all were von Braun's Saturn rockets that carried the Apollo astronauts to the Moon.

and shot it into the air. The neighbors called the police. Soon after that, Goddard moved to New Mexico to test his rockets in the empty desert. Goddard developed a way to control a rocket to keep it upright, better ways to cool rocket engines, and faster and more powerful rocket designs. In 1935 he fired a rocket that went faster than the speed of sound, and another that reached a height of 7,500 feet (2,300 m)!

While Robert Goddard imagined rockets traveling to the Moon someday, others were thinking of a very different, more immediate use for them. When World War II started, military leaders wanted rockets that could deliver more than weather instruments. They wanted rockets to carry weapons.

ROCKETS FROM WAR TO SPACE

During the 1930s there were a number of rocket clubs around the world that built and experimented with rockets. The German Society for Space Travel became a famous rocket club. One of its members was a physicist named Hermann Oberth. Oberth's 1923 book, *The Rocket into Interplanetary Space*, inspired many researchers'

interest in rockets. In fact, it caused a 13-year-old boy to study harder in school so he could understand the book's math. That boy was Wernher von Braun, who would become one of the world's most important rocket engineers.

As a young man of 18 in 1930, von Braun joined the German Society for Space Travel and began assisting Oberth in testing the motors of liquid-fueled rockets. Within a few years the German government outlawed rocket testing by civilians. But by then von Braun was doing research for the German army. In 1942 he led the team that launched the world's first rocket capable of carrying explosives to distant targets—a ballistic missile. It was so powerful that it reached the fringes of space.

Von Braun's successful launch caught the attention of Germany's leader, Adolf Hitler. By 1944 Germany was launching the V-2 rocket to its target 350 miles (560 km) away: England. When the first V-2 "vengeance weapon" hit London, Wernher von Braun commented, "The rocket worked perfectly except for landing on the wrong planet." The Nazis would fire more than 3,000 V-2s at England before the

Walk to Pluto

Why did it take so long to find Pluto? Because it's a small world and it's really far away! How far? Find out for yourself by walking the relative distances between the planets and dwarf planets below. You'll need a big park or a long street to make it all the way to Pluto! Pick an easy-to-see landmark (such as a goal post or a building) as your starting point, the Sun. You can use rocks or friends as markers for each world along the way.

TO GET FROM	WALK THIS MANY STEPS
Sun to Mercury	3
Mercury to Venus	2½
Venus to Earth	2
Earth to Mars	4
Mars to Jupiter	27½
Jupiter to Saturn	32½
Saturn to Uranus	72
Uranus to Neptune	81½
Neptune to Pluto	71

BONUS: Want to walk on to Eris, the newly discovered dwarf planet? From Pluto you'll need to walk 512 steps to reach Eris's place in space.

This German V-2 rocket launches from its new American home in New Mexico in 1946.

Sergei Korolev (1906–1966)

Sergei Korolev in 1954, with a dog that had just ridden into space on a rocket.

Sergei Pavlovich Korolev was an aeronautical engineer who built missiles for the USSR during World War II. In 1945 Korolev traveled to defeated Germany, learned the V-2's secrets, and then copied them to build the USSR's R-7 rocket.

Sergei Korolev founded the Soviet space program and made the USSR the world's first space-faring nation. Korolev's rockets carried the first person into space. His spacecraft were the first to impact, orbit, and photograph the Moon. And Korolev's designs were used to create the first space probe to reach another planet. Sadly, Sergei Korolev died from a botched surgical operation during the height of his career. Because the Soviet space program was so secretive, Korolev wasn't really known or recognized until years after his death.

war ended. More than 2,750 people were killed and thousands more wounded by V-2s.

Von Braun and his team of rocket scientists knew that, despite the V-2 attacks, Germany was losing the war. The scientists decided to hide their priceless rocket designs from the German army and surrender to the Americans, offering their knowledge in exchange for safe haven. In 1945 von Braun and 116 other German rocket scientists turned themselves over to the United States Army. General Dwight D. Eisenhower's plan was to obtain the scientists' experiment records, files, scientific data, and test vehicles, and to put the German scientists to work for the United States. "Operation Paperclip," as this secret plan was called, worked exactly as Eisenhower had hoped. The scientists, their families, and a number of captured V-2 rockets were moved from Germany to New Mexico, where rocket laboratories were set up. Some of the best rocket scientists in the world were now improving their rockets and building missiles for America.

The U.S. government wanted a rocket program for military reasons. They wanted rockets that could carry nuclear weapons across the ocean or even around the world. As General Henry H. Arnold commented in 1945, "The next war will not start with a naval action nor . . . by aircraft flown by human beings. It might very well start with missiles being dropped on the capital of a country, say Washington."

But the same rockets that carried weapons could also explore space, too, scientists hoped. Project Bumper was a plan to stack one rocket on top of another. This plan marked the beginning of multistage rocketry. The idea was to use one of von Braun's V-2 rockets to get the multistage rocket off the ground. Once in the air, the V-2 rocket would drop away and a second rocket would ignite and carry the vehicle even higher. The second rocket was called a WAC Corporal. It was built for the army by the Jet Propulsion Laboratory (JPL). On February 24, 1949, the world's first multistage rocket was launched. The Bumper rocket reached a speed of 5,250 miles (8,450 km) per hour and flew 244 miles (400 km) into space. That's the height of some space shuttle flights! The Earth's gravity no longer trapped humanity—space was ours to explore.

THE SPACE RACE STARTS UP

The Soviets might not have captured von Braun, but they'd gotten a few German rocket scientists of their own after the war. The Soviets had a robust rocket program and a brilliant Russian rocket designer, Sergei Korolev. Korolev had been experimenting with rockets since the early 1930s. He and other Soviet rocket scientists spent much of World War II under arrest and in labor camps. But the brutal Soviet leader Joseph Stalin wanted missiles, so Stalin allowed the scientists to work while imprisoned. Korolev and his team quickly copied, then improved upon, the V-2 rocket. Soon they were working on Korolev's rocket masterpiece, the R-7. It would be the first rocket able to deliver a weapon to another continent. The R-7 was the world's first intercontinental ballistic missile (ICBM).

Meanwhile, scientists around the world wanted rockets for another reason besides missiles. The year 1957–1958 had been declared International Geophysical Year. The idea was to promote international scientific study of Earth's upper atmosphere and outer space during an upcoming time of intense solar activity that

Rocket Anatomy

Rockets are classified by their propellants, or fuel. Liquid-fuel rockets use kerosene, gasoline, or some other liquid fuel along with a separate liquid oxidizer. Solid-fuel rockets have their oxidizer mixed in as part of the solid propellant. In rockets with multiple stages (including most space-bound rockets), some stages use liquid rockets while others use solid rockets.

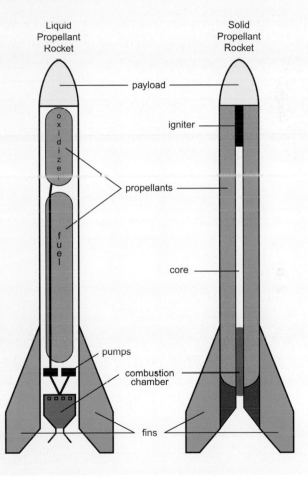

would include solar flares. In 1955 U.S. President Dwight D. Eisenhower made a startling announcement: the United States was building the world's first artificial satellite, and it planned to launch the satellite during the upcoming International Geophysical Year. Even more shocking, a month later the Soviets announced that the USSR would beat the United States to the punch: it would be the one to launch the world's first artificial satellite. The space race was on.

While Korolev worked on his R-7 rocket in the USSR, von Braun worked on America's ICBM, the Redstone rocket. But when the time came for President Eisenhower to choose a rocket to launch the promised U.S. satellite, he didn't pick von Braun's Redstone. Instead, he chose the Vanguard rocket being developed by the U.S. Navy. By the middle of 1957 the Vanguard project was in full swing. When, in September, the Soviets announced that they'd soon be sending up a satellite to orbit Earth, almost everyone thought the Soviets' statement was just ridiculous propaganda. How could the Soviets be farther along than the Americans who'd captured von Braun's rocket team? Unfortunately, no one

outside the USSR knew anything about the Soviet rocket program. It was top secret. The rest of the world had no clue that the Soviets weren't bluffing or propagandizing. Few suspected the truth—the USSR really was ready to launch the world's first satellite.

THE SPUTNIK SURPRISE

On the night of October 4, 1957, a section of the Kazakh Desert in Kazakhstan, in central Asia, was full of giant floodlights. On the lit launchpad was an R-7 rocket. Inside the rocket's payload, or storage area, was a round, shiny metal object

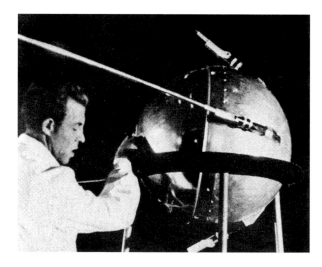

Above are the radio transmitter and other instruments inside *Sputnik 1*'s outer sphere of aluminum alloy. At left, a Soviet technician readies *Sputnik 1* for its 1957 launch.

about the size of a basketball that weighed 183 pounds (83 kg). It was a satellite (*sputnik* in Russian). Korolev listened to the countdown from the command bunker. His eyes nervously darted from one set of instruments to another. With the shout of "liftoff" ringing in Korolev's ears, the engines ignited. The 300-ton (273,000-kg) booster blazed and smoked, and the R-7's five engines pushed the rocket into the night sky.

The Soviet scientists and engineers quickly gathered around their radio equipment. They would soon know if the rocket had successfully released the little satellite into orbit. Soon they heard a sound on the radio: "beep-beep-beep . . . beep-beep-beep . . . beep-beep-beep." It had made it! Cheers and congratulations went out. *Sputnik 1* was the first artificial object to orbit the Earth. The USSR was the first country in space. The importance of the event didn't seem to hit the current Soviet leader at first. Premier Nikita Khrushchev said, "They phoned me that the rocket had taken the right course and that the satellite was already revolving around the Earth. I congratulated the entire group of engineers . . . and calmly went to bed."

Above left, *Sputnik 2* awaits launch in November 1957. Its payload is the dog Laika, the first earthling in orbit. Above right is a Moscow museum display showing how Laika traveled.

Leaders in the United States were not as calm. For 23 days *Sputnik 1* beeped on radios and twinkled like a fast-moving star as it orbited the Earth every 98 minutes. All of America saw it in the October 1957 night sky. How and when had the Soviets developed this technology, the U.S. government wondered? They worried that, if the Soviets had a rocket that could carry a satellite to space, they surely also had one that could send a nuclear weapon to America. Before the shock of *Sputnik 1* wore off, a month later the Soviets launched its much larger *Sputnik 2*. This proved that the Soviets had rockets more powerful than America's. And even more unbelievably, *Sputnik 2* carried a living passenger. A dog named Laika (which means "barker" in Russian) had become the first earthling in orbit. She not only weathered the rocket trip, but she lived for a number of days in orbit. Laika proved that living beings could survive in the microgravity of space if they were provided oxygen. What was to keep humans from going there now?

THE UNITED STATES PLAYS CATCH-UP

What was keeping the Americans from getting to space? A rocket that worked! Still reeling with shock over Sputnik, the U.S. Navy prepared to launch a better-late-than-never U.S. satellite with its Vanguard rocket. On December 6, 1957, at Cape Canaveral, Florida, the Vanguard rocket was ignited. Two seconds later it exploded in a giant ball of fire. U.S. President Eisenhower called in his pinch hitter—von Braun.

Von Braun had been waiting to prove that his rocket was space ready. Now he got that chance. Von Braun's team needed to transform their Redstone missile into a rocket that could launch a satellite into space—a launch vehicle. It only took them 84 days to do it. The result was Juno 1, a four-stage, 72-foot-tall (22-m-tall) rocket. Juno 1 lifted off from Cape Canaveral on January 31, 1958. On board was a small,

The test of the Vanguard TV3 rocket in December 1957 ended in disaster. The U.S. Navy–built rocket exploded on the launchpad.

seven-foot (2-m) satellite called *Explorer 1*. After separating from Juno 1, *Explorer 1* went into orbit, making its highest pass 1,580 miles (2,550 km) above the Earth.

The United States came in second in this first round of the space race. But while *Explorer 1* wasn't first, it did result in some important scientific discoveries. Instruments aboard the satellite measured the temperature out in space and found a belt of radiation in the atmosphere between 620 and 3,000 miles

Go Satellite Watching activity

The rockets that carried the first U.S. satellites into orbit were basically military missiles that were loaded with payloads instead of weapons. Above, a Redstone missile sits on the launchpad in 1958. At left, a modified Redstone is assembled into a Juno 1 (also called a Jupiter-C) launch vehicle in 1958.

The whole world looked up at the night sky in October 1957. *Sputnik 1* sped across the sky, outpacing all the stars as it circled Earth. Today the night sky is a much busier place. There are all kinds of weather, communications, and scientific satellites orbiting Earth these days—as well as space telescopes, the International Space Station, and sometimes a space shuttle.

On a clear night in a dark place, try to spot some of these satellites and orbiting spacecraft in the sky. Sit or stand facing south toward the equator, where most satellites orbit. Look for small, steady points of white light moving really quickly across the sky. (Blinking lights or red lights are from jets or airplanes, not orbiting satellites or spacecraft.) Most satellites will first appear over the western horizon (on your right), speed across the sky, and disappear over the eastern horizon (on your left) in just a few minutes. So look sharp! Some satellites orbit over the Earth's poles instead of the equator. To see these, find the North Star and look at what's cruising by it. (To find the North Star, first look for the Big Dipper. The two stars that make up the Big Dipper's pouring edge point to the bright, unmoving North Star.)

The International Space Station is one of the most visible objects in the night sky. The NASA Web site http://spaceflight1.nasa.gov/realdata/sightings as well as a number of the sky calendar Web sites listed on page 165, can tell you if and when it will pass over your city.

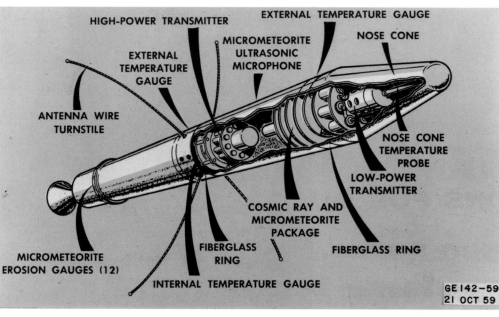

HIGH-POWER TRANSMITTER
EXTERNAL TEMPERATURE GAUGE
EXTERNAL TEMPERATURE GAUGE
MICROMETEORITE ULTRASONIC MICROPHONE
NOSE CONE
ANTENNA WIRE TURNSTILE
NOSE CONE TEMPERATURE PROBE
LOW-POWER TRANSMITTER
COSMIC RAY AND MICROMETEORITE PACKAGE
MICROMETEORITE EROSION GAUGES (12)
FIBERGLASS RING
FIBERGLASS RING
INTERNAL TEMPERATURE GAUGE
GE 142–59
21 OCT 59

Left: technicians install the first successful U.S. satellite, *Explorer 1*, atop its launch vehicle in 1958. The diagram (above) shows the satellite's scientific instruments.

(1,000 and 5,000 km) up—the Van Allen belt. *Explorer 1* stopped transmitting data after about a month. In February 1958 the United States tried another Vanguard launch. The rocket broke up in flight. The Soviets were also having problems. That same month, the launch of a third Sputnik by the USSR failed as well. On March 2, the United States suffered another blow when its *Explorer 2* failed to orbit. Getting to space was proving tricky.

Both the United States and the Soviet Union kept firing satellite-toting rockets into the sky all through the spring and early summer of 1958. Only one of the six Vanguard launches attempted by the United States in 1958 was successful, and two of its five Explorers failed to

After the successful launch (at right) of *Explorer 1*, a model of the first U.S. satellite was triumphantly displayed to the public. Celebrating the launch (left): William Pickering, the director of JPL, which built *Explorer 1*, is on the left. James van Allen, in the center, designed and built *Explorer 1*'s instrument that identified the radiation belts. Wernher von Braun is on the right.

orbit. By the end of International Geophysical Year, the United States space program had a success rate of about 36 percent. The USSR had a 75-percent success rate—and they'd flown a dog to space. How could the United States catch up? The U.S. Congress boosted funding for government science projects, as well as for math and science education. On July 29, 1958,

President Eisenhower signed the National Aeronautics and Space Act. It called for a new civilian—not military—space agency, and it stated that "activities in space should be devoted to peaceful purposes for the benefit of all mankind." Two months later the National Aeronautics and Space Administration was formed. NASA opened for business.

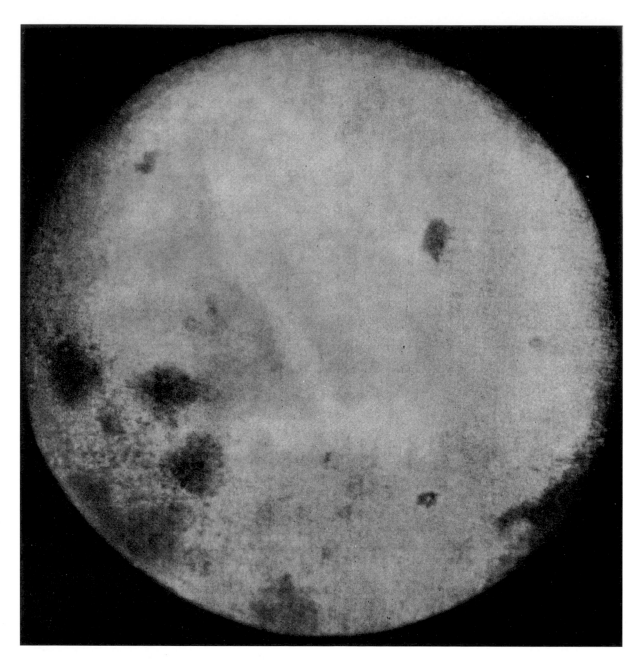

SHOOTING FOR THE MOON

The Soviet Sputniks and American Explorers proved that rockets could deliver Earth-orbiting satellites to space. But the rockets, or launch vehicles, carrying those satellites didn't completely break Earth's gravitational grip. They hadn't reached escape velocity, or the speed required to escape the Earth's pull. The next step was to overcome the pull of our planet and head into the unexplored solar system. Where should these first space probes be sent? The Moon seemed like the perfect target.

The United States took the first shot at reaching the Moon. Engineers packed a probe (see sidebar on page 47) named *Pioneer 0* with a television camera and other scientific equipment and launched it in August 1958. A little more than a minute after liftoff, *Pioneer 0* exploded. Chunks of the launch vehicle crashed into the ocean. Two months later, NASA launched its first spacecraft, *Pioneer 1*. But the new space agency would know failure before

This was the first glimpse ever of the far side of the Moon. The picture was taken by the USSR's *Luna 3* lunar probe in 1959.

Pioneer 4 was NASA's first successful mission to the Moon in 1959.

success. While NASA sent *Pioneer 1, 2,* and *3* toward the Moon in 1958, none reached escape velocity or made it to the Moon. What happened? Each had problems with one or more of the stages of the launch vehicle igniting when it was supposed to, or how it was supposed to.

Meanwhile, the Soviets weren't reaching the Moon in 1958 either. Their first three attempts at sending lunar probes failed, too. But the new year of 1959 brought the Soviets better luck. In January 1959 the USSR's *Luna 1* reached escape velocity, separated from the launch vehicle's third stage, and headed toward the Moon. After traveling 70,200 miles (113,000 km) from Earth, the Soviet lunar probe released a cloud of sodium gas. The glowing orange trail created by the gas was seen by astronomers on Earth as it sparkled over the Indian Ocean. *Luna 1* had become an artificial comet! A day later *Luna 1* reached (though didn't touch) the Moon, flying by it within 4,000 miles (6,400 km). The historic

probe then went into orbit around the Sun, where it remains today.

The Soviets' *Luna 1* was the first human-made object to reach escape velocity, the first space-craft to reach the Moon, the first lunar flyby probe, and the first artificial object to orbit the Sun. Once again coming in second, NASA had its first lunar success with *Pioneer 4* in March 1959. America's first flyby probe flew by the Moon, but didn't get close enough to take pictures, as NASA had planned. Six months later the USSR's *Luna 2* became the first spacecraft to touch the Moon. It hit the surface and scattered Soviet emblems and ribbons across the surface of another world. And on October 7, 1959, *Luna 3* flew by the Moon and sent back another first. The probe snapped pictures of something no human had ever seen before—the far side of the Moon, which is always turned away from Earth. A space probe from Earth gave humans a look at something in the solar system they had never before seen. It would be the first of many new, miraculous sights.

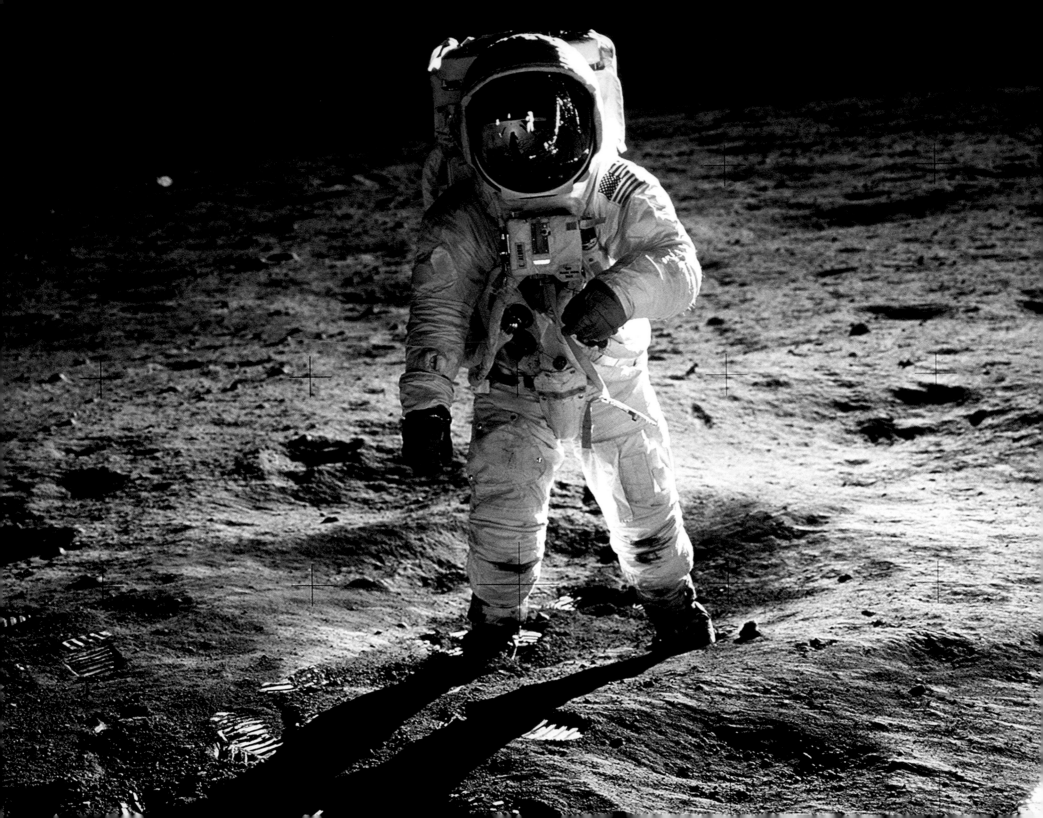

3

1960s: Racing to the Moon—and Beyond

A s the 1960s began, the space race was no longer just about who could launch the best missile-carrying rockets or spy satellites. Nor was it only a contest between the United States and the Soviet Union to see who could get robotic spacecraft on the Moon and beyond first. Some scientists and pilots weren't settling for exploring the solar system in a secondhand way. They wanted to see for themselves what was beyond our small blue planet. But was it even possible for people to survive a trip into outer space? Could humans become space travelers?

SPACE SAILORS

As it had with Sputnik and Luna, the USSR again took the early lead in the race to carry earthlings into space. Soviet dogs Belka and Strelka followed in Laika's pawsteps in 1960. *Sputnik 5* carried the two dogs—along with 40 mice, 2 rats, and a bunch of plants—around the Earth 18 times. But unlike unfortunate Laika, the dogs Belka and Strelka returned to Earth. Their special recovery capsule parachuted safely to the ground after falling through the atmosphere. In fact, all of

Buzz Aldrin on the Moon in 1969.

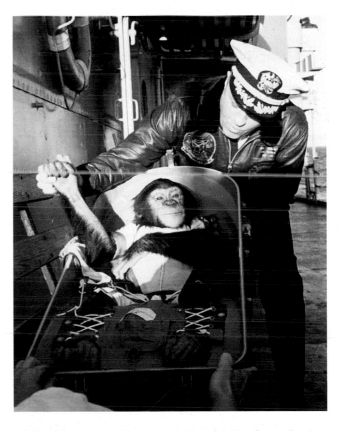

NASA chimpanzee Ham gets a handshake from the Commander of his recovery ship after his Mercury capsule spaceflight in 1961.

NASA's first astronauts, the Mercury Seven. Front row from left: Walter Schirra, Donald Slayton, John Glenn, and Scott Carpenter. Back row from left: Alan Shepard, Gus Grissom, and Gordon Cooper.

the *Sputnik 5* space animals survived, proving that round-trip space flights were possible.

While the USSR continued to send canines into space, the United States instead drafted monkeys and chimps for the job. In January 1961 a chimpanzee named Ham flew into space in a U.S. Mercury capsule. Ham safely splashed down in the ocean inside his Mercury capsule, no worse for wear. Project Mercury's three goals were to put "a manned spacecraft in orbital flight around the earth; Investigate man's performance capabilities and his ability to function in the environment of space; and recover the man and the spacecraft safely." The first seven candidates chosen by NASA to travel to space were called the Mercury Seven. All seven were military test pilots. NASA called them astronauts, which means "sailors of the stars." Not to be outdone, the USSR also began

selecting Soviet pilots to be its "sailors of the universe," or cosmonauts. So who'd get to be the first certified space sailor—an astronaut or a cosmonaut?

YURI'S BIG DAY

Yuri Gagarin awoke in the early morning hours of April 12, 1961, to a doctor shaking his shoulder. Twenty-seven-year-old Gagarin wasn't in the hospital, but he wasn't at home, either. The room he'd slept in was on the grounds of Baikonur, the secret Soviet space launch site in remote Kazakhstan. Gagarin smiled and jumped out of bed when he remembered where he was—and why. Today was the day the Soviet air force pilot would sail the cosmos and become a true cosmonaut.

After eating a hearty breakfast of pureed meat with toast and jam, Gagarin suited up and rode a bus over to the launch site. There he climbed into the *Vostok 1* spacecraft and strapped into his padded seat. At 9:55 A.M., about 100 feet (30 m) below Gagarin, the giant rocket began to rumble. The nearly five-ton (4,500 kg) spacecraft slowly rose up over the

The first Soviet cosmonaut group. Front row from left: Pavel Popovich, Viktor Gorbatko, Yevgeniy Khrunov, Yuri Gagarin, Chief Designer Sergei Korolev, his wife Nina Korolev (holding Popovich's daughter Natasha), Training Director Yevgeniy Karpov, parachute trainer Nikolay Nikitin, and physician Yevgeniy Fedorov. Middle row from left: Alexei Leonov, Andrian Nikolayev, Mars Rafikov, Dmitriy Zaykin, Boris Volynov, Gherman Titov, Grigoriy Nelyubov, Valeriy Bykovskiy, and Georgiy Shonin. Back row from left: Valentin Filatyev, Ivan Anikeyev, and Pavel Belyayeu.

launchpad and Gagarin yelled out, "Off we go!" before he was squashed breathless against his seat by the force of liftoff. Less than a minute later Gagarin was traveling faster than the speed of sound and unable to move his arms or legs. Suddenly, Gagarin lurched forward against his restraining straps as the *Vostok 1* slowed for an instant. The booster rockets shut off, disconnected with a hollow-sounding clunk, and dropped away. Then the second stage fired,

slamming Gagarin back against his seat. After two more lurch-and-slam rocket stage changes, Gagarin cleared the atmosphere. He felt the engine shut down as *Vostok 1* fell into orbit around the Earth. The cosmonaut's notebook, pencil, and arms rose up into the air of the cockpit. Gagarin was floating in the microgravity of space!

Yuri Gagarin looked out the spacecraft's porthole window. "I see Earth. It's so beautiful!" Gagarin radioed back to Earth. They were the first words spoken from a human in space. When Gagarin saw Africa from his window he realized that his single loop around the Earth was almost over. The retro-rockets soon fired and *Vostok 1* began falling through Earth's atmosphere. When he was about 13,000 feet (4 km) above the USSR, Gagarin ejected from the capsule and parachuted safely to the ground. An elderly villager, her granddaughter, and a cow were the first earthlings to greet Yuri Gagarin. By the end of the day, however, most of the world knew his name. Yuri Gagarin was the first human in space.

The president of the United States was not happy that the first person in space was a

Yuri Gagarin (1934–1968)

Yuri Gagarin was born on a collective farm in Russia. The Nazis invaded his small village during World War II, and young Gagarin's family was forced to live in a dirt dugout. While under German occupation, Gagarin witnessed airplane battles between the Nazis and red-starred Soviet fighters. On his ninth birthday, those same red-starred soldiers liberated Gagarin's village. When he grew up, Gagarin joined the Soviet air force.

After *Luna 1* flew to the Moon in 1959, Gagarin volunteered to go into space. He was accepted into the new cosmonaut corps and after training was picked to make the first space flight. On April 12, 1961, Yuri Gagarin orbited once around the Earth, becoming the first human in space. But it would be Yuri Gagarin's only trip into space. He trained other cosmonauts in the early 1960s and was in line to pilot the *Soyuz 3* mission. Tragically, before he could return to space, Gagarin was killed in an airplane accident.

cosmonaut, not an astronaut. It didn't seem to matter that Mercury astronaut Alan Shepard made a non-orbiting space flight three weeks after Gagarin had shot into space. President John F. Kennedy was tired of the Soviets always getting there first! What could America do to take the lead in the space race? NASA leaders gave Kennedy their answer. "With a strong effort," reported NASA, the United States might be able to land a man on the Moon before the Soviets. Perfect. President Kennedy spoke to the U.S. Congress on May 25, 1961, explaining his Cold War reasoning for a Moon mission. He said, "If we are to win the battle that is now going on around the world between freedom and tyranny, the dramatic achievements in space which occurred in recent weeks should have made clear to us all, as did the *Sputnik* in 1957, the impact of this adventure on the minds of men everywhere, who are attempting to make

Yuri Gagarin (top) rides to the launchpad before his historic 1961 flight, which made newspaper headlines around the world (at left). Notice Wernher von Braun's quote on the front page: "To keep up, U.S.A. must run like hell."

a determination of which road they should take. . . . I believe that this nation should commit itself to achieving the goal, before this decade is out, of landing a man on the Moon and returning him safely to the Earth. No single space project in this period will be more impressive to mankind, or more important for the long-range exploration of space; and none will be so difficult or expensive to accomplish." The race to the Moon was on!

LUNAR LEARNING

To some, the idea of putting a person on the Moon before 1970 seemed crazy. To many others, it seemed simply impossible. When President Kennedy made his historic 1961 announcement, only a single American had ever been in space. And Mercury astronaut Alan Shepard had only spent 15 minutes there! NASA hadn't had much success with robotic space probes (see sidebar on 47), either. Of the six Moon probes that had been launched by NASA at that point, *Pioneer 4* was the sole successful lunar probe. And *Pioneer 4*'s journey had been far from perfect, flying by the Moon at a much

greater distance from it than planned. How was NASA ever going to set a crew-carrying spacecraft safely down on the Moon, allow humans to walk around on the surface, and get the astronauts back to Earth alive?

NASA planned to accomplish the Moon landing project by focusing on two specific plans of attack. The first was Project Gemini. This astronaut program was designed to bridge the gigantic gap between Project Mercury and the Apollo Program, which was created to send a man to the Moon. It was in the Gemini missions that scientists demonstrated how astronauts could survive and work in space. Gemini missions also developed and tested spacecraft that could orbit, maneuver, dock, land, and relaunch. Project Gemini was both a lunar spacecraft test lab and an astronaut boot camp.

The second plan of attack was to gather more information about Apollo's destination. NASA needed to know more about the Moon and its surface so it could decide where, exactly, to safely land the spacecraft. This job was done by robotic space probes. The first series of probes were called the Ranger fleet, and they weren't

NASA astronaut Alan Shepard being hoisted aboard a helicopter after his *Freedom 7* Mercury space capsule splashed into the ocean on May 5, 1961.

Map the Moon's Surface

activity

You don't have to board a spacecraft to explore the surface of another world in our solar system. You can see the Moon's mountains, plains, valleys, and craters from Earth!

Not all phases of the Moon are created equal when it comes to seeing lunar surface details. The new Moon is too dark, of course. But the brightness of the full Moon washes out many lunar details. The best times for seeing the Moon clearly are around the quarter phases. You'll see the best detail of the right-hand side of the Moon's surface during the first-quarter phase, and the best detail of the left-hand side during the third-quarter phase.

YOU'LL NEED

Binoculars

Pencil or pen

Paper

Moon phase calendar (available on most wall calendars, in the weather section of newspapers, on weather-related Web sites, or on the sky calendar Web sites listed on page 165)

1. Find the Moon in the night sky during its first-quarter or third-quarter phase. You can observe the Moon outdoors or through a window in a dark room.
2. Focus the binoculars on the Moon. What can you see on the lit half? The large dark patches are ancient lava seas or plains, which are called maria. The lighter-colored areas are covered in craters and mountains.

3. Draw the features you see on your paper, creating a map of half the Moon. Use the map below to help you label what you see.
4. Repeat steps 1–3 during the opposite Moon phase two weeks later to map the other half of the lunar surface.

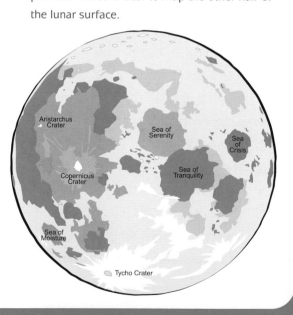

Aristarchus Crater

Sea of Serenity

Sea of Crisis

Copernicus Crater

Sea of Tranquility

Sea of Moisture

Tycho Crater

terribly successful. Of Ranger's nine launches, the first six didn't succeed. The rocket launch vehicle failed in the first two attempts; the probe itself failed on the third attempt, causing *Ranger 3* to miss the Moon; the computer on *Ranger 4* failed to send back any data; the power system on *Ranger 5* failed, causing that probe to miss the Moon as well; and, although *Ranger 6* did make it to the Moon, its cameras failed and it crash-landed without sending back any pictures! *Ranger 7* finally broke NASA's string of failures. In 1964 the seventh probe made it to the Moon and sent back 4,316 sharp pictures of the lunar surface. *Ranger 8* and *Ranger 9* were also successful, and they gave scientists a view of the Moon that was a thousand times more detailed than what could be seen through telescopes. The Ranger pictures showed fields of gray dust, rocks, and craters within craters. Was the dust like snow? Did it hide deep, dangerous craters beneath it like snow-covered crevasses? Would a spacecraft sink into the dust and not be able to lift off again? Could a moonwalking astronaut fall into a deep, dust-covered hole and disappear?

The Surveyor lander probes were sent to find out. NASA sent seven Surveyors to the Moon between 1966 and 1968. Each was a 625-pound (283-kg) lander full of instruments and cameras on a tubular frame that was perched on three shock-absorbing footpads. Five of the Surveyor landers made successful soft landings on the lunar surface, taking pictures and scooping up soil and rocks and photographing them. *Surveyor 7* sent back pictures showing rocks that had once been molten! This indicated that the Moon must have once had active volcanoes and flowing lava. Earth's moon had its own secret past.

To test landings, *Surveyor 6* set down, lifted off ten feet (3 m) into the air, then safely landed again a few feet away. The first landing didn't leave a big hole. Lunar dust wasn't quicksand. The Moon's surface was solid. A spacecraft could definitely land on it—but where, exactly? To survey and scout for the perfect landing site, NASA sent five lunar orbiters to the Moon during the years that the Surveyor landers were being sent there as well. All the missions were successful, and by the time the last lunar orbiter had completed its job in early 1968, more than

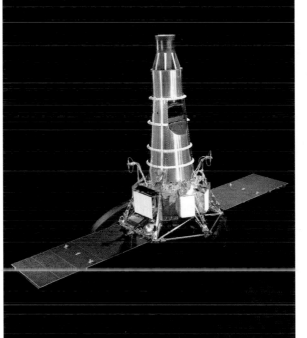

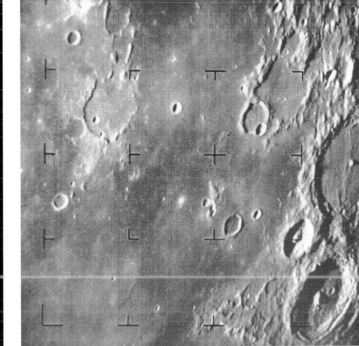

Ranger 7 was the first U.S. spacecraft to take a picture of the Moon in 1964.

99 percent of the Moon's surface had been mapped. NASA now knew where to land to avoid dangerous craters and big boulder fields. The orbiters also looked for meteoroids and checked the radiation levels so that the Apollo spacecraft and spacesuits could be built to protect the astronauts. While NASA would welcome any

new discoveries about the Moon thanks to Apollo, they also wanted the astronauts to know exactly what they were getting into. Surprises could be dangerous. The Ranger, Surveyor, and Lunar Orbiter missions took the guesswork out of where Apollo astronauts would land and what they'd find on the Moon.

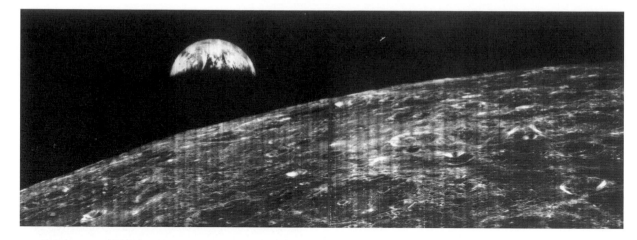

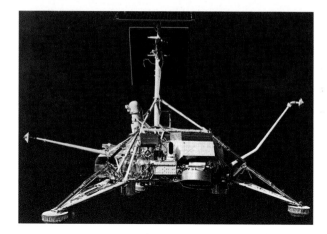

Five Surveyor landers like this one (bottom) set down on the Moon between 1966 and 1968, while the same number of Lunar Orbiters mapped the Moon's surface. *Lunar Orbiter 1* snapped this first view of Earth from lunar orbit (top).

SOVIET SUCCESSES AND TRAGIC FIRSTS

While NASA furiously worked to achieve its goal of putting astronauts on the Moon, the Soviet space program continued to outpace America, racking up "space firsts" in both human space-flight and lunar exploration. The USSR's Gherman Titov spent the first full day in orbit aboard *Vostok 2*—six months before John Glenn made three orbits in early 1962. *Vostok 3* and *Vostok 4* took part in the world's first dual-spacecraft mission later that same year. Soviet space firsts continued in 1963 as cosmonaut Valeriy Bykovskiy spent a phenomenal five days in orbit in *Vostok 5*. Bykovskiy returned to Earth on June 19, the same day that *Vostok 6* brought Valentina Tereshkova back. She was the first

woman in space. Sally Ride became the first American woman in space two decades later.

As NASA's Project Mercury evolved into Project Gemini, so did the Soviet's Vostok pro-gram change to Voskhod. Like Gemini, the goal of the Voskhod program was to produce and test spacecrafts that could go farther, carry more cosmonauts, and dock with each other. (It's no coincidence that these were all necessary elements for a crewed lunar landing.) Three cosmonauts crammed into *Voskhod 1* and made the first multi-person spaceflight in 1964. And Alexei Leonov made the first space walk outside *Voskhod 2* in 1965.

While the Voskhod program focused on developing and improving cosmonaut-carrying spacecraft, the Soviets' Luna probe program kept collecting information about the Moon— and racking up more Soviet space firsts. *Luna 9* became the first successful lunar lander, setting down on the Moon four months before NASA's *Surveyor 1* did in 1966. And later that same year *Luna 10* became the first probe to orbit the Moon. *Luna 10* completed 460 orbits in a little over four months, just as NASA launched its equivalent probe, *Lunar Orbiter 1*.

Space Probes

A space probe is a robotic space explorer. It's a crewless spacecraft that collects information and takes images of the solar system and sends both the information and the images back to Earth. Space probes go where humans can't. They bring the solar system to us—via a stream of radioed data.

Space probes come in a variety of sizes and kinds. Each space probe is designed for its own particular job and interplanetary destination. There are six basic kinds of space probes:

- A **flyby probe** makes observations, snaps pictures, and collects information as it flies by the planet. Flyby probes aren't near the planet for a long time, and they only observe the part of the planet they are flying by. But they are the simplest and cheapest probes to send, and one probe can fly by more than one planet. Some famous flyby probes are *Luna 3*, *Mariner 4*, *Pioneer 10*, *Pioneer 11*, *Voyager 1*, and *Voyager 2*.

- An **orbiter** places itself in an orbit around a planet (or moon) for a long time—often years. Over time the orbiter can observe, photograph, and map a planet's entire surface. And, because it often orbits over the same area more than once, orbiters can record and track changes on the planet. *Mariner 9, Mars Global Surveyor, Magellan,* and *Cassini* are famously successful orbiters.

- An **atmospheric probe** is a package of instruments that travels through the atmosphere of a planet. It collects weather information and other data until it hits the surface, burns up, or is crushed by atmospheric pressure. *Venera 4* was an atmospheric probe, and *Pioneer 12*, *Pioneer 13* (later renamed *Pioneer Venus 1* and *Pioneer Venus 2*), and *Galileo* released atmospheric probes.

- A **lander** sets down on a planet or moon to take close-up photographs, analyze soil samples, and observe the surface in detail. Some famous first landers include *Luna 9, Venera 7,* and *Mars 3*.

- A **rover** is a robot vehicle that roams across the surface. It usually does tasks that are similar to those performed by a lander, but rovers aren't stuck in one spot. *Lunokhod 1*, *Lunokhod 2*, *Sojourner*, *Spirit*, and *Opportunity* were rovers.

- A **sample-return** space probe collects a sample and delivers it back to Earth. That sample can be rocks or soil from a planet, moon, or asteroid. Or the sample can be tiny particles from comet tails or the solar wind. *Lunas 16, 20,* and *24* returned samples from the Moon. *Genesis* collected and returned solar wind particles. *Stardust* delivered its collected comet tail particles in 2006.

Not all missions involve just one kind of space probe. Many spacecraft are loaded with more than one type of probe. Spacecraft that are orbiters might also release a lander or an atmospheric probe toward the surface of the planet or moon they are orbiting. Likewise, some landers carry rovers on board.

In 1967 both the United States and the Soviet Union continued to scout and survey the Moon with probes. These orbiters and landers collected information on landing sites and searched for any unwelcome surprises that might foil future cosmonauts and astronauts. Meanwhile, both countries' human spaceflight projects were throwing off their training wheels. Project Gemini was finished, and Apollo, the U.S. Moon landing program, had begun. The Soviets also moved on to their next program— Soyuz. Each country felt a lot of pressure to push ahead quickly. The "end of the decade" deadline loomed over NASA and both nations felt the fierce Cold War competition. Perhaps it was all too much, too fast. The tragedies of 1967 would prove that speedy progress had been substituted for safety in the space race.

The first space disaster of 1967 happened on the ground. The very first Apollo mission ended before it left Earth. A short in the wiring of the *Apollo 1* capsule caused a spark during a test run. The pure-oxygen environment of the *Apollo 1* cabin transformed that spark into an inferno within seconds. Three NASA astronauts—Gus

Grissom, Ed White, and Roger Chaffee—died inside the *Apollo 1* capsule before the hatch could be opened on January 26, 1967. Three months later, disaster struck the Soviets as well. Cosmonaut Vladimir Komarov died when his *Soyuz 1* capsule crashed during reentry. The first-of-its-kind Soviet capsule spun wildly as it descended, fatally tangling its parachute lines. The Soviets had tragically earned another space first—the first person to die during spaceflight.

SUPER ROCKET AND REHEARSALS ON TV

The *Apollo 1* fire put the astronaut part of the Apollo program on hold while the spacecraft was redesigned. (The Soviets did the same with Soyuz.) But Apollo's launch vehicle was ready to go. So NASA went ahead and launched *Apollo 4* without astronauts in late 1967. It was quite a sight. The Apollo launch vehicle was an enormous three-stage rocket. Wernher von Braun had designed it to take astronauts on a half-million-mile (800,000-km) journey to the Moon. It's difficult to exaggerate Saturn V's size, power, and complexity. It was the biggest, most

The remains of the *Apollo 1* capsule after a fire killed three astronauts.

powerful rocket ever built—and it still is. It was taller than the Statue of Liberty. Even though it weighed more than six million pounds (2.8 million kg) it could still push both itself and a large spacecraft out of Earth's gravity grip! The first and second stages of the Saturn V had five engines each. Inside the rocket was a maze of three million parts, including pumps, gauges, circuits, switches, sensors, and fuel lines. When the first stage of Saturn V ignited under *Apollo 4*, the ground shook under the spectators' feet. The first five engines created such a roaring noise that nothing else could be heard. It was like a miraculous monster coming to life.

Why such a gigantic, super-booster Moon rocket? A lunar-landing spacecraft with astronauts aboard needed a big launch vehicle to travel so far and to accomplish such a complex task. When NASA was given the goal of landing astronauts on the Moon, there was no single spacecraft that could fly there, land, take off again, and return to Earth. So NASA decided on a lunar orbiting rendezvous, or LOR, mission. The mission called for a three-part spacecraft made up of Command, Service, and Lunar

The *Apollo 8* astronauts photographed Earth as they orbited the Moon in 1968.

modules (see diagram at right). All three parts would travel together to the Moon. The combined Command/Service Module (CSM) would orbit the Moon while the Lunar Module (LM) set down on the surface. Von Braun was given the job of building a rocket big enough to carry all three modules—and three astronauts—to the Moon.

The first launch of the Saturn V was a monumental success. The crewless *Apollo 4* CSM splashed down in the Pacific Ocean after a nine-and-a-half-hour flight. After two more successful crewless test runs, NASA decided that *Apollo 7* would carry astronauts into space in October 1968. The astronauts spent 11 long days in Earth's orbit as they put the Apollo modules through the paces. Their most serious problem was suffering through bad head colds.

Next up were the *Apollo 8* astronauts. They successfully launched atop a Saturn V rocket two months later, flew to the Moon, and orbited it 10 times. *Apollo 8* astronauts Frank Borman, Jim Lovell, and William Anders became the first humans to travel at escape velocity, the first to travel to the Moon, and the first to see the

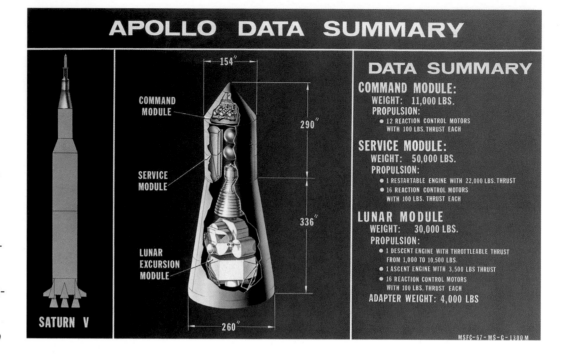

entire Earth from space. "We see the Earth now, almost as a disk," reported Borman. "We have a beautiful view of Florida now," added Lovell. The astronauts shared their magnificent views and experiences with everyone on Earth during four TV broadcasts before coming home on December 27, 1968. Surely astronauts would land on the Moon by the end of the decade now!

NASA's efforts at lunar learning and mission planning were paying off. Each step that successfully tested a technology brought another

piece into place. The Saturn V rocket could go all the way to the Moon. Orbiting the Moon had been done, too. *Apollo 9* tested the docking maneuvers needed for a lunar-landing mission with success. *Apollo 10* was the last puzzle piece. Its three astronauts made a final rehearsal flight to the Moon in May 1969. *Apollo 10* flew to the Moon, and its Lunar Module separated from the CSM and flew down to within 50,000 feet (15,240 m) of the Moon's gray surface before successfully returning to Earth. Now every aspect of landing on the Moon had been practiced. NASA finally gave its Moon landing project an official name. The spacecraft that would carry the first humans to another world and land there would be *Apollo 11*.

LANDING ON THE MOON

A billion people watched *Apollo 11* launch on July 16, 1969, from Kennedy Space Center in Florida. It roared into the sky, spewing fire and smoke. The ride atop a gigantic rocket as it plows through air and clouds isn't smooth. But the jerking and shaking trip to Earth's orbit took only 12 minutes. After two and a half hours of circling their home planet, astronauts Neil Armstrong, Mike Collins, and Buzz Aldrin were ready to go. The third stage of the Saturn V kicked in, and *Apollo 11* broke orbit and began its trip to the Moon.

Once away from Earth, the *Apollo 11* astronauts inside Command Service Module *Columbia* separated from the rocket, turned completely around, and docked on Landing Module *Eagle*. The maneuver went perfectly—just like they'd practiced! The third stage of the rocket fell away

as planned, and the *Columbia* and the *Eagle*, which were now joined together, sped on through space. After three days of seeing nothing but stars and darkness, the astronauts caught their first glimpse of the Moon. As its image filled the hatch window, Commander Armstrong commented that it was "a view worth the price of the trip." *Apollo 11* had reached the Moon. The *Columbia-Eagle* slowed and went into lunar orbit about 70 miles (113 km) above its surface, circling every couple of hours as the astronauts got ready for their next step—landing on the Moon.

On July 20 astronauts Armstrong and Aldrin opened the docking hatch between CSM *Columbia* and LM *Eagle* and climbed into the lander. Collins's job was to keep *Columbia* in orbit around the Moon. "I'll see you cats later,"

Wernher von Braun and his Saturn V rocket getting ready for the *Apollo 11* launch.

Collins said with a smile. Once inside the *Eagle* lander, Aldrin and Armstrong undocked from *Columbia* and headed down toward the Moon. As they neared the lunar surface, *Eagle* slowed down. Armstrong and Aldrin monitored their instruments as the onboard computer executed *Eagle*'s landing as planned. From their window, the astronauts caught site of the Moon's Sea of Tranquility in the distance. Like other maria, it looked like a dark, smooth plain—a perfect landing site.

When *Eagle* was a little more than a mile (2 km) above the gray surface an alarm light flashed on. Mission Control in Houston told the astronauts not to worry. The ship's computer was a bit overloaded, but *Eagle* was still a "go" for landing. Six more alarm lights flashed, keeping Aldrin and Armstrong busy in the following minutes as they worked to identify and solve the problems. But when they next looked out the window, they realized they had an even bigger problem. Their landing site was actually in the middle of a bunch of boulders! If the *Eagle* crashed during landing it wouldn't be able to take off again. And there was no way for the

Official portrait of the *Apollo 11* lunar landing mission crew. From left to right: Commander Neil Armstrong, Command Service Module Pilot Michael Collins, and Lunar Module Pilot Buzz Aldrin.

orbiting *Columbia* to get them off the Moon. Aldrin and Armstrong would be stranded there until their oxygen ran out, and then they would die. The surface was coming up fast now— it was less than 2,000 feet (610 m) away.

Neil Armstrong didn't so much think as simply react to the situation. His lifelong experience as a pilot had prepared him to act fast in potentially life-threatening situations. Armstrong had received his pilot's license on his 16th birthday.

He'd flown in 78 combat missions (and been shot down) during the Korean War. Armstrong had more than a thousand flight hours under his belt as a test pilot of supersonic fighters and the X-15 rocket plane. And he'd safely piloted *Gemini 8* from outer space to an emergency splashdown in the Pacific. When Armstrong saw the *Eagle* in danger of crash landing, the pilot in him automatically reacted—and took control.

Armstrong quickly switched to manual control and accelerated *Eagle* away from the boulder field. A "low fuel" warning alarm immediately lit up. Armstrong needed to either land *Eagle* in the next minute or abort the landing completely; otherwise, they wouldn't have enough fuel to get back to the *Columbia*. Armstrong saw a clear spot of land sandwiched between some boulders and craters. It was only the size of a house, but it would have to do. With only 20 seconds' worth of fuel left, Armstrong gently set the *Eagle* down on the Moon's surface, right in the small clear spot that he'd found. "Houston, Tranquility Base here," Armstrong called to Mission Control. "The *Eagle* has landed." Cheers of joy—and relief—went up at Mission Control. They'd done it!

Astronaut Buzz Aldrin, working on the Moon outside the *Eagle* lander during the *Apollo 11* mission in 1969.

EXPLORING THE MOON FIRSTHAND

As he uttered the famous words, "That's one small step for a man, one giant leap for mankind," Neil Armstrong created the first footprints on the Moon. He didn't sink into deep dust or fall into a hole, as some had worried. "The surface is fine and powdery," reported Armstrong. "It's actually no trouble to walk around." Buzz Aldrin soon joined Armstrong on the Moon, describing the black sky and gray surface as "beautiful, beautiful, magnificent desolation." Then the astronauts went to work collecting moon rocks, setting up science experiments, and snapping pictures. Their equipment recorded gentle moonquakes, collected solar wind particles, and sent a laser beam of light back to Earth. Before heading back to re-dock with *Columbia*, the astronauts planted an American flag and left a plaque that says, "Here men from the planet Earth first set foot upon the Moon, July 1969 A.D. We came in peace for all mankind."

The astronauts of the *Apollo 11* mission made history. They were the first humans on the

Commander Eugene Cernan drives a lunar roving vehicle during the *Apollo 17* mission in 1972.

Moon! But the *Eagle* was there for less than a day, and Armstrong's and Aldrin's moonwalk had lasted less than three hours. Fortunately, the astronauts in the following Apollo missions had more time for exploration—and experimentation—on the Moon. *Apollo 12* launched four months later and set down in the Ocean of Storms, near the spot where *Surveyor 3* had

landed two years earlier. The astronauts documented and collected 75 pounds (34 kg) of rock, soil, and core samples during two four-hour moonwalks. Most of the samples they collected were dark volcanic rocks, called basalts, that turned out to be hundreds of millions of years younger than the rocks collected during the *Apollo 11* mission.

Unlucky *Apollo 13* didn't make it to the Moon after an explosion ("Houston, we've had a problem here") turned the mission into a fight for the astronauts' survival. Fortunately, as the movie *Apollo 13* shows, they made it home safely. *Apollo 14* took up *13*'s aborted landing site, setting down in the Fra Mauro region in early 1971. Alan Shepard, the first American in space, and Stuart Roosa hauled samples on a two-wheeled trolley while hiking and climbing the highland area. The men collected more than 98 pounds (44 kg) of rock and soil during nine hours of moonwalks.

Apollo 15 astronauts had it easier, thanks to the new lunar roving vehicle they'd brought along. The *Apollo 15* astronauts roved around the Hadley Rille section of the Moon in style for three days! CSM *Endeavor* pilot Alfred Worden had his own excitement during the *Apollo 15* mission. He became the first person beyond Earth's orbit to spacewalk. *Apollo 16* took astronauts to an area of the Moon that was completely different from the broad flat maria that the previous missions had visited. They landed in the light-colored Descartes Highlands

Geologist Harrison Schmitt scoops up lunar soil (above) to take back to Earth. One of the many moon rocks (left) collected during *Apollo 17*.

Work Like an Astronaut

activity

The Apollo astronauts didn't travel to the Moon just to jump around in low gravity and put up flags. They also did a number of experiments and collected lots of moon rock and soil samples. But working in a big, bulky spacesuit isn't easy. Get a feel for what it's like to work in a lunar spacesuit in this activity.

YOU'LL NEED

Oversized jacket, coat, or heavy long-sleeved shirt

Newspaper or tissue paper

Gloves that fit you snugly

Oversized heavy work gloves

Large bolt and a nut that fits it

Jar or plastic container with lid

Pennies

Small cup

1. Put on the oversized jacket. Ask a friend or family member to help you stuff crumpled newspaper or tissue paper into the sleeves up to your shoulder. It should be difficult to move your arms!
2. Put on the snug-fitting gloves. Then put on the oversized work gloves over them. Your spacesuit is complete.
3. Now get to work! Try to do some simple tasks, like opening and closing a jar or plastic container, fitting a nut onto a bolt, and putting pennies into a cup. What's especially hard to do? Why?

on April 21, 1972. During 20 hours of moonwalks, the astronauts collected a record 213 pounds (96.5 kg) of samples and roved some 17 miles (27 km). They discovered that the Descartes Crater was magnetized, and they took moonquake measurements.

The final Apollo Moon mission was one of the most exciting for scientists—especially for one particular scientist, a geologist named Harrison "Jack" Schmitt. Schmitt is the only scientist ever to walk on the Moon. Schmitt, Commander Eugene Cernan, and CSM pilot Ron Evans left Earth aboard *Apollo 17* on December 7, 1972. Cernan and Schmitt landed in the Taurus-Littrow Valley with more scientific instruments than any other Apollo mission. During their first trip out of the lander, the astronauts set up an automated research station, as well as instruments to measure lunar gravity and atmosphere. During a second, seven-hour moonwalk, Cernan and Schmitt discovered a weird orange soil while roving a few miles south of the lander. The Moon's chemical makeup is the cause of the soil's odd color.

On Schmitt and Cernan's third day on the Moon, the astronauts roved out to the northeast part of the valley. On the way they discovered a split boulder, and they stopped to take core samples from a crater's rim. Then they returned to the LM *Challenger* to get ready to head back home. But before Apollo astronauts left the Moon for the last time, they placed a plaque on its surface. The plaque reads: "Here man completed his first explorations of the Moon December 1972, A.D. May the spirit of peace in which we came be reflected in the lives of all mankind."

The Apollo Program landed a total of 12 humans on another world for the first—and, so far, only—time in history. NASA's Moon missions were miracles of technology, and the methods and instruments used during these missions would also be used in future robotic space probe missions beyond the Moon. And, while the United States sprinted to the Moon to beat its Soviet rival in the space race, Apollo was more than just a Cold War weapon. We learned much of what we today know about the Moon thanks to Apollo. The astronauts brought back more than

841 pounds (381.5 kg) of lunar samples. These moon rocks, bags of dust, and core samples were shared with hundreds of waiting scientists throughout the world. Amazing discoveries were uncovered in the lunar samples. One moon rock contained water and another held a never-before-seen mineral made of titanium, iron, and magnesium oxide. The newly discovered type of mineral was named armalcolite after Armstrong, Aldrin, and Collins.

Information collected during the Apollo missions and from the samples the astronauts brought back completely changed what we know about the familiar object in the night sky. The Moon, it turns out, is not just an old hunk of space rock. It's its own world, with its own history of volcanoes, moonquakes, and meteorite impacts. Its youngest rocks are as old as Earth's oldest rocks. And while it's certain that the Earth and its moon share a common ancestry, the Moon never had what is needed to form an atmosphere, have surface water, and produce life. There may not be life on the Moon, but at least life has now visited there.

Harrison "Jack" Schmitt (b. 1935)

Harrison Schmitt grew up in Silver City, New Mexico, a great place for rock hounds. After becoming a geologist, Schmitt developed moon rock-collecting techniques for the Apollo astronauts. Then Schmitt decided he'd like to go to the Moon himself! NASA selected him as part of its first scientist-astronaut group.

Unlike the early astronauts, Schmitt wasn't a military pilot. But he trained on simulators for both the LM and the CSM. After *Apollo 17* splashed down in late 1972, Schmitt helped document Apollo's geologic findings. Schmitt left NASA in 1975 and was elected to a term in the United States Senate. Today he runs a company called Interlune Intermars Initiative, Inc. that promotes going back to the Moon for good. "Humans need to find other places in the solar system to live," says Schmitt. "A permanent return to the Moon will be as significant as our early ancestors' migrations out of Africa."

The Soviet *Lunokhod 3* rover.

ROBOTIC ROVERS ON THE MOON

The Soviet space program never did put a cosmo-naut on the Moon. The USSR cancelled its clan-destine lunar cosmonaut program after *Apollo 11*'s success. But that didn't stop the Soviets from collecting their own lunar samples. In 1970 the Soviet probe *Luna 16* landed on the Moon, scooped up some lunar soil, and launched it back to the USSR—simply astounding! *Luna 16* was the first successful robotic sample-return mission. Sample-return missions are still very rare today.

Later that same year the Soviets made history again. The USSR sent a robotic rover to the Moon on *Luna 17* in late 1970. The first robot to rove on another world was named *Lunokhod 1*, which means "moonwalker" in Russian. The 2,000-pound (900-kg) wonder wheeled around on the Moon for nearly an entire year! The Lunokhod rovers of the early 1970s were some of the Soviet lunar exploration program's greatest successes. Robotic rovers and crewless probes would prove to be the way of the future. Humans wouldn't be exploring the solar system beyond the Moon firsthand anytime soon. Visiting the planets would be a job left to space probes.

FLYING BY OUR NEIGHBORS

Venus and Mars are Earth's nearest planetary neighbors. And, not surprisingly, they were the first to be visited by robotic spacecraft. The Soviets shot space probes toward Mars as early as 1960—three years after *Sputnik 1*—and toward Venus in 1961. But none of these earliest spacecraft made it. NASA had its own first failures sending space probes to the planets. *Mariner 1* failed during its launch toward Venus in 1962. But another Mariner probe would succeed in 1962 and earn the United States another space first.

In August 1962 many of the scientists at NASA were puzzling out how to get astronauts on the Moon. But NASA's Jet Propulsion Laboratory instead spent the Apollo years designing 10 spacecraft to visit other planets. They named these the Mariner spacecraft. On August 27, 1962, NASA launched *Mariner 2* atop an Atlas rocket. After reaching space, the 441-pound (200-kg) solar-powered probe headed toward Earth's sister planet, Venus. It would take three and a half months to get there. On the journey to Venus, *Mariner 2* measured solar wind and

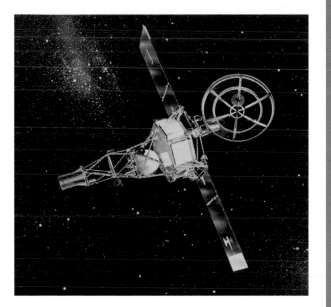

Venus visitor *Mariner 2* was the world's first interplanetary spacecraft.

interplanetary dust. (Space turned out to be less dusty than scientists had expected.) *Mariner 2* also detected solar flares on the Sun and cosmic rays coming from beyond our solar system.

December 14, 1962, was the big day. *Mariner 2* arrived at Venus, becoming the first spacecraft to visit another planet. *Mariner 2* flew by Venus, passing within 21,600 miles (34,762 km) of its mysterious surface. As the probe flew by, its instruments scanned the planet. These scans showed that Venus spins slowly—and backward!

Create Kitchen Craters

activity

The Moon is covered with craters. They are impact craters that were caused by meteors, asteroids, and comets slamming into its surface. Some of the Moon's impact craters are big, deep, and perfectly round. Others are smaller, shallower, and not so round. Find out what gives a crater its shape in this activity.

YOU'LL NEED

Newspaper

9" x 13" (23-cm x 33-cm) baking pan

6 cups (.8 kg) flour

6 cups (1.8 kg) salt

Spatula

2 tablespoons (13 g) paprika, cinnamon, or cocoa powder

3 different "impactors" such as a marble, a stone, and a rock, shell, or coin

Tongs

1. Spread newspaper on the floor. Set the baking pan on the newspaper.
2. Fill the pan with the salt and flour and mix together. This is your "lunar soil." Use the spatula to smooth out the top of the soil.
3. Sprinkle a thin layer of paprika, cinnamon, or cocoa across the lunar soil. This will help your craters show up better. Your lunar landscape is ready for impact!
4. Hold one of the impactors about 12 inches (30 cm) above one side of your moonscape. Drop it into the lunar soil.
5. Repeat step 4 with the other 2 impactors. How are the three craters different? What created the deepest crater? The widest? The oddest shaped?
6. Use the tongs to carefully remove the impactors from their craters. Then ask a friend of family member to try to match each impactor with the crater it created. Good luck!

(It takes Venus longer to spin around once—243 Earth days—than to make one trip around the Sun. That means Venus's day is longer than its year!) And *Mariner 2*'s infrared radiometer discovered that Venus's thick cloud covering and carbon dioxide atmosphere are like a blanket, creating temperatures four times hotter than scientists had predicted. The scalding surface is 900°F (480°C). Venus may be Earth's twin in size, but *Mariner 2* shattered any theory that its climate was similar to ours.

Another Mariner probe became the first spacecraft to visit Mars. *Mariner 4* reached the Red Planet in July 1965 after a voyage of nearly eight months. Unlike *Mariner 2*, *Mariner 4* had a camera, and it sent the first pictures of another planet back to Earth. Each of *Mariner 4*'s 21 precious pictures of Mars took 25 minutes to transmit! Unfortunately, what those pictures showed disappointed many people.

Scientists had long hoped that Mars harbored life. Ever since astronomers started peering through telescopes, some had reported seeing canals or riverbeds on the planet's surface. And even modern telescopes showed a Martian surface that changed colors with the seasons. Surely at least primitive plants—or *something* that was alive—called Mars home. But *Mariner 4* failed to snap any images of Martians of any kind. The photos showed no indications of life on Mars at all: no people, no animals, no plants, no canals—not even any water. In fact, the black-and-white photos showed a dead, dry, cratered world that looked very much like the Moon. Mars was declared lifeless.

But these first space probes offered only quick, fly-by glances at our nearest neighbor worlds. They gave an incomplete picture at best and an inaccurate one at worst. *Mariner 4* photographed only 1 percent of Mars. It would be up to future space probes to discover its canyons, dry riverbeds, and icy poles that today indicate that there was once water—and perhaps life—on Mars.

Many more discoveries were yet to come. As the Apollo missions wound down, the golden age of planetary exploration began. Humans would learn more about their solar system during the 1970s than they had in the previous thousand years.

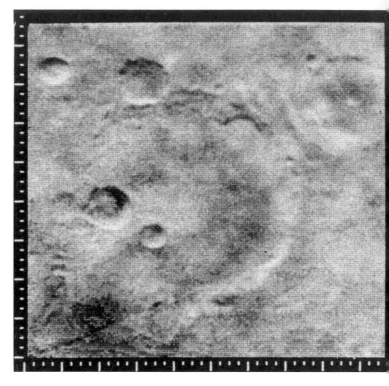

This is one of the first pictures of Mars ever taken by a spacecraft. The cratered surface shown in *Mariner 4*'s black-and-white images looked more like the Moon than Mars to many.

How the Space Race Was Won

How did NASA astronauts beat Soviet cosmonauts to the Moon? Remember that for the first 10 years of spaceflight the USSR outpaced the United States. Starting with Sputnik, the Soviets collected one space first after another. So how did NASA catch up and beat the Soviets to the Moon? The short answer is the Saturn V. The Soviet's equivalent super-booster N-1 moon rocket kept exploding during tests. NASA got to the Moon before the Soviets solved the N-1's problems.

Why the Soviets couldn't perfect their moon rocket in time is more complicated. The world knew very little about the workings of the Soviet space program back then. It was run by the USSR's secretive military. Failed missions weren't reported—or even named. The Soviets had never even publicly declared that they were trying to put cosmonauts on the Moon. But why else would they build a rocket big enough to carry a crew there? Much of what we now know about the Soviet space program has been learned since the USSR dissolved in the early 1990s.

Today we know that the two Cold Warrior nations ran the space race in very different ways. The Soviet space program struggled for resources from the start. When Sergei Korolev (see page 28) was designing the first Soviet space rockets after World War II, he had trouble getting the parts and metals that were needed. Those involved in the Soviet space program learned to depend on simpler technologies and materials from the start. For example, Soviet spacecraft were made of stainless steel instead of the lighter-weight (but more expensive) titanium and aluminum that NASA used. And while NASA was so high-tech that it even developed a pen with ink that flowed in microgravity, cosmonauts simply used pencils. Some of NASA's high-tech advances—such as the space pen—didn't really make much of a difference in the race to space. But others, like the materials and technology used to build the Saturn V, did matter. Just using lighter-weight metals, for example, can make the difference between a rocket that can lift off and one that can't.

Fewer resources also meant that the Soviets couldn't do as much testing and made for riskier launches and flights. One catastrophic accident that set the Soviet space program back happened in 1960, though no one outside of the USSR knew about it until decades later. The so-called Nedelin disaster killed more than 100 Soviet scientists and technicians when the rocket they were working on exploded on the launchpad. The Soviet press didn't report the accident. Instead, the obituaries of a few rocket technicians simply turned up in the press every month or so. It took two and a half years for all those who'd died in the Nedelin disaster to be reported dead. Today a memorial stands in memory of their lost lives.

Another big loss to the Soviet space program was the shocking early death of rocket engineer Sergei Korolev in 1966. If he and the rocket scientists who died in the Nedelin disaster had lived, the space race might have ended very differently.

1970s: Probing the Planets

4

Viking 2 **on Mars in 1976.**

The 1970s were a golden age of space exploration through the use of planet-bound space probes (see sidebar on page 47). NASA launched a dozen successful spacecraft toward the planets between 1971 and 1978. And the Soviets sent their share of planetary visitors, too. (See the Field Guide time lines starting on page 138.) These spacecraft eventually visited all eight planets in the solar system. The probes sent back pictures and made discoveries that forever changed what we know about the solar system—and our place in it.

Unbelievably, what's today considered the golden age of planetary exploration nearly ended before it began! The space race between the United States and the USSR had fueled the space program during the 1960s. But after *Apollo 11*'s triumph on the Moon, interest cooled and money became harder to get. In the first years of the 1970s, the U.S. Congress slashed NASA's budget. Apollo missions 18, 19, and 20 were canceled. And human spaceflight missions weren't the only ones cut. Scientists at NASA wanted to use big rockets, such as the Saturn V moon rocket, to send large space-

craft packed with science instruments to Jupiter, Saturn, Neptune, Uranus, and Pluto. These missions were to be called the Grand Tour missions. But the program was declared too extravagant and expensive, and it was denied funding. NASA would have to make do with smaller, Mariner-style spacecraft instead.

EARLY VISITS TO MARS AND VENUS

The Grand Tour might have been canceled, but both NASA and the Soviets continued to send spacecraft to explore the nearby planets. Early on, the USSR took the lead in the exploration of Venus, and the United States took the lead in missions to Mars. Both nations pushed ahead, wanting to do more than just fly by the planets and snap a few pictures. Scientists had figured out how to orbit and land robotic spacecraft on the Moon. Now they had to transfer that technology to planetary missions. But other planets are much farther away than the Moon. Were small space probes up to the challenge of traveling the long distances? And planets had other obstacles the Moon didn't have—such as thick atmospheres, windy

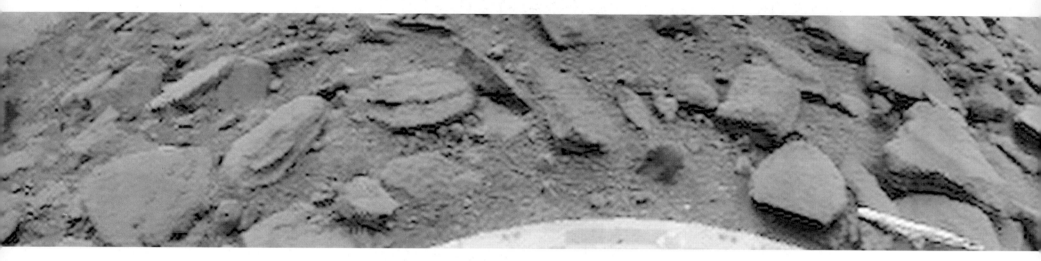

The Soviet lander *Venera 9* took this picture of Venus's surface in 1975.

weather, and who knew what else! Could the probes handle those, too?

In 1970 the USSR's *Venera 7* became the first spacecraft to successfully set down on another planet. Cosmonauts might not have made it to the Moon, but a Soviet spacecraft landed on Venus! *Venera 7* broadcast data back to Earth for 23 minutes before Venus's lead-melting temperatures shut it down. The USSR sent more than a dozen successful missions to Venus during the 1970s and 1980s. *Venera 9* and *Venera 10* radioed back the first photos of Venus's surface. They showed a pebbled plain of rocks, which had once been lava, illuminated by fuzzy light seeping through the thick overhead clouds. Amazing!

Space scientists were soon designing probes to do more and more. NASA wanted to explore Mars in depth, not just fly by it again as *Mariner*s 4, 6, and 7 had. The black-and-white snapshots from those Mariners showed a cratered, lifeless world. Would orbiters that could carefully scan the entire surface of Mars find something different, something more interesting? In May 1971 NASA scientists readied two Mars orbiters, *Mariner 8* and *Mariner 9*.

Mariner 8 was first up for launch. It left the pad, but the second stage of its launch vehicle blew up, and *Mariner 8* fell into the Atlantic Ocean. The *Mariner 9* team had only weeks to figure out what had gone wrong with the rocket and fix it before the next launch. They did, and *Mariner 9* was successfully sent on its six-month journey toward Mars. It became the first spacecraft to orbit another planet.

It's a good thing that *Mariner 9* was an orbiter. If it had been a flyby probe, the *Mariner 9* mission would have failed. Why? In September, while *Mariner 9* traveled toward Mars, astronomers on Earth noticed something odd. Telescopes pointed at Mars showed a yellow cloud forming in its southern hemisphere. Soon all of Mars was engulfed in a planet-wide dust storm with 400-mile-per-hour (645-km-per-hour) winds. It was the largest storm ever observed on Mars—and *Mariner 9* was headed right for it! When the 2,200-pound (998 kg) *Mariner 9* arrived at Mars in November, its cameras couldn't pick up much through the storm—just four odd dark blotches in the Northern Hemisphere. But because it was an orbiter, *Mariner 9* was able to

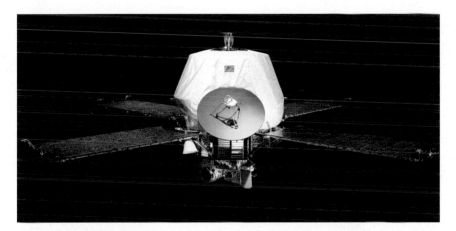

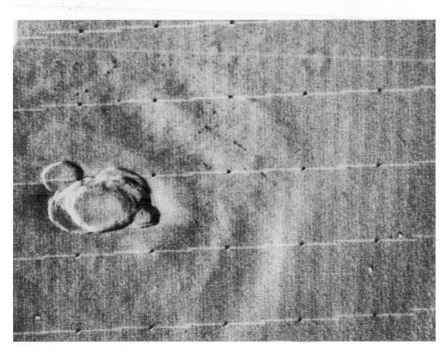

Mariner 9 (top) took this picture (bottom) of the giant crater atop the volcano Olympus Mons on Mars in 1971.

Planetary Warm-Up activity

Venus is the hottest planet in the solar system. Why? Its thick carbon-dioxide atmosphere soaks up heat and radiates it back to the planet. You can see how different colors, like different kinds of atmospheres, soak up heat in this activity.

YOU'LL NEED

2 thermometers

2 glass or plastic bottles of equal capacity, 1 green and 1 clear

2 bottle caps, corks, or balls of modeling clay that fit the mouths of the bottles

1. Set a thermometer inside each bottle. Put the bottle caps on the bottles, or seal them with corks or a ball of clay. Make sure they're well sealed!
2. Leave the bottles in a sunny window. Make sure that both bottles are in direct sunlight and that neither is casting a shadow on the other.
3. After an hour, read the temperature in each bottle. Which is warmer? Why?

simply start circling the Red Planet and wait out the storm. The view turned out to be well worth the wait. Once the dust died down it became apparent that those four dark blotches were actually the tops of gigantic, never-before-seen volcanoes! The biggest one, Olympus Mons, is more than three times as tall as Earth's highest mountain peak, and it has a base so wide that it'd cover all of Missouri! But Mars doesn't only have the largest known mountain in the solar system. *Mariner 9*'s pictures showed that it also has the largest canyon. Valles Marineris is a canyon so long that it would stretch clear across the United States. *Mariner 9* radioed back more than 7,000 amazing images as it orbited Mars for nine months. Its pictures completely changed scientists' thoughts about Mars. It isn't a long-dead, cratered world. Mars is a geologic wonder full of dry river channels and ancient landslides that hint that water once flowed there. *Mariner 9*'s findings whetted NASA's appetite for an even closer look at Mars. A mission to send landers to look for life on Mars was soon on the drawing boards. That mission was called Viking.

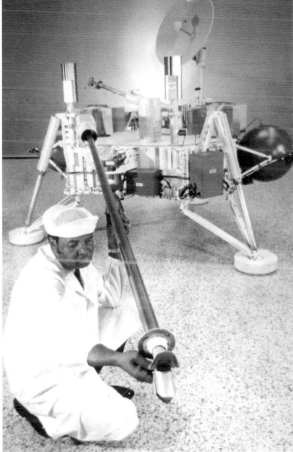

This early rendering of the Viking Project illustrated how each spacecraft would release its lander while the orbiter continued to circle Mars (left). A technician checks the soil sampler of the Viking lander (above) before launch.

LIFE ON MARS?

The Mars-focused Viking Project would be NASA's most sophisticated program of planetary exploration yet. It took nearly a decade of planning and the work of hundreds of scientists, engineers, technicians, administrators, and support staff to get the twin orbiter-lander *Viking 1* and *Viking 2* spacecraft to Mars. Once there, the orbiters would map Mars's surface from space and the landers would look for life on the ground. But just how does a robotic lander look for life? It was Jerry Soffen's job to figure that out.

Jerry Soffen led the science team that designed the first experiments on the surface of Mars. Soffen and his Viking Project team of 70 scientists came up with a laundry list of experiments, tests, and observations they wanted the landers to do on Mars. But at the top of the list was the question of life. Is—or was—there life on Mars? It was a question that Jerry Soffen had wondered about for many years. Soffen wasn't an engineer or a mathematician. He was a biologist, a life scientist. While in college during the 1950s, he became fascinated with theories

An astrobiologist works on the miniature robotic Viking laboratory.

about the origin of life on Earth. After all, it was also the "origins of me," commented Soffen.

Then the Sputnik program happened, and soon afterward came human spaceflight. People were actually going to explore the planets and search for extraterrestrial life! Jerry Soffen wanted to be part of it, so he became an exobiologist, a scientist who studies life on other planets. Soffen joined the Jet Propulsion Laboratory, working on science instruments that could detect life for spacecraft. It was perfect practice for the Viking Project.

Soffen and his Viking Project science team turned the Viking landers into robotic scientists. Each Viking lander carried a weather station, a seismograph for detecting quakes, two computers, a photo lab, a soil-scooping robot arm, a trench-digging shovel, a conveyor belt to move collected soil into mini-labs for analysis, and equipment to communicate with Earth. All of this was packed into a tough little three-legged lander that was about the size of a golf cart! That left a space about the size of a toaster for the automated life-detection and chemistry labs inside each of the landers' bellies. Soffen and his team had to create miniature versions of high-tech equipment that would be able to do things such as grind up soil, separate and identify gases, and even mix soil with nutrients to see if anything grew. Everything was shrunk down in size, again and again, so it'd all fit. The tubes that carried the gases were as thin as hair! And it all had to work on its own, on the surface of another world millions of miles away.

ROBOT SCIENTISTS ON MARS

Once the landers were finished being built, they were sterilized before being packed with their orbiters into launch vehicles. Sterilization kills any stowaway Earth microbes that might contaminate Mars or be mistaken later as Martian life. *Viking 1* was launched on August 20, 1975, and *Viking 2* took off on September 9, 1975. Ten months later, *Viking 1* was orbiting the Red Planet. NASA had studied photos taken by *Mariner 9* to pick out a landing site for *Viking 1*'s lander. But *Viking 1*'s camera, which was better than that on *Mariner 9*, showed the landing site

Is It Organic?

activity

Would you recognize life on another planet if you saw it? One way scientists look for the possibility of life in the solar system is by testing for organic compounds. All life on Earth—whether animal, plant, bacteria, or fungus—contains the element carbon. Chemical compounds that contain carbon are called organic compounds, and they are often associated with life. So looking for organic compounds is standard procedure for space probes. Find out if you can tell an organic compound from an inorganic (not organic) one.

YOU'LL NEED

Scissors (optional)

Piece of white paper

Microwave oven

Pencil

Pinch of white sugar

Pinch of salt

Magnifying glass (optional)

1. Cut or tear the paper so that it just fits in the microwave without touching the sides. If your microwave oven rotates the food on an inner plate as it cooks, just make sure the paper doesn't go over the plate edges.

2. Write the words "sugar" and "salt" at opposite ends of one side of the paper. Put the pinch of salt near its label, and do the same with an equal-sized pinch of sugar.

3. Look carefully at the sugar and salt samples. Use the magnifying glass, if you have one, to study them. How are they different? How are they the same?

4. Carefully place the paper in the microwave oven, and turn the oven on high for five minutes. Let the paper cool down first, then study the samples again. Has one of them changed? If not, continue to heat them on high, one minute at a time, until one of the samples changes. What happens?

5. Let the paper cool down. Then examine the samples carefully again. Which one is organic? How can you tell?

Viking 1 **lander on Chryse Planitia. The rock is named Big Joe.**

This picture shows the *Viking 2* lander scooping up soil to be tested inside its science lab.

to be dangerously rough and rocky. Thank goodness for the orbiter! NASA quickly put it to work searching for a better landing site. NASA decided on an area called Chryse Planitia, which means "golden plains." On July 20, 1976, the *Viking 1* lander separated from the orbiter, fired a retrorocket to break orbit, and began its descent to Mars. After deploying a parachute and firing more retro-rockets, *Viking 1* was slowed to 5 miles (8 km) per hour and set down softly on the sands of Mars, seven years to the day after *Apollo 11* landed on the Moon.

Later that very same day the first pictures of the Martian surface arrived back on Earth. The color photographs showed a desert scene of rocks and rusty soil beneath a pink sky. Jerry Soffen was thrilled. "Mars had become a place," he explained. Soffen likened it to seeing a friend's pictures of his or her trip climbing Mount Everest. Knowing someone personally who's gone somewhere exotic can make it seem more real. "[*Viking 1*] was not a person, but he was a close friend," Soffen said.

Viking 2 set down just as elegantly 4,000 miles (6,437 km) away at Utopia Planitia. Both landers got to work right away. The first weather broadcast from Mars reported a light wind and a chilly afternoon temperature of -21°F (-29°C). It wasn't T-shirt weather! The soil analysis reported an iron-rich clay that constantly oxidized, or rusted, giving it a red color. Except for a fussy seismometer, all the science instruments worked well. "How remarkable!" said Soffen. "We are performing chemical and biological experiments as though in our own laboratories. Taking pictures at will, listening for seismic shocks, and making measurements of the atmosphere and surface—all of this from the first spacecraft ever to be landed successfully on Mars."

Meanwhile, the twin Viking orbiters were also hard at work. They mapped 97 percent of the Martian surface and photographed both Martian moons. Some of the more than 50,000 images taken by the orbiters were so close up and clear that features as small as houses could be seen. The Mars that was revealed by the orbiters was a varied place with erosion, volcanoes, and what looked like evidence of ancient lakes and rivers long since gone dry. The orbiters also confirmed that the ice of the polar ice cap was

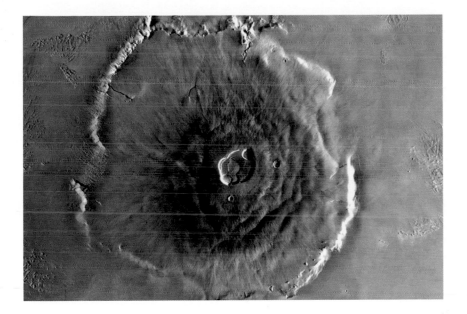

made from water, not carbon dioxide ("dry ice") as was once thought. And the orbiters found an element in the upper atmosphere that many claimed was required for life—nitrogen.

The main job of the landers was to look for life on Mars. The landers dug trenches in the soil and then their robotic arms scooped up a sample. Conveyors carried the soil into the landers' mini-laboratories for analysis. Once inside the labs, the soil was mixed with water, nutrients, and other chemicals, and the results were recorded. If bacteria or other life forms were in the soil, the mini-labs would detect them.

They didn't—at least nothing conclusive. Carl Sagan used to say, "Extraordinary claims require extraordinary evidence." The Viking landers found no such extraordinary evidence that anything lived on Mars. Soffen, like many others, was disappointed. The thin atmosphere allowed so much ultraviolet radiation to hit the surface that it pretty much sterilized the soil, said Soffen. Maybe there was life further underground, out of the reach of so much radiation and nearer the ice caps, where

The twin Viking orbiters mapped 97 percent of Mars, giving us the best view of the Red Planet yet. Notice the ice cap (above) and the detailed view of Olympus Mons (left).

Carl Sagan (1934–1996)

As a boy, Carl Sagan often wondered about the lights in the night sky. Years later, Sagan was studying planetary astronomy when the Soviets launched *Sputnik 1*. Sagan started working for NASA, briefing Moon-bound Apollo astronauts and working on the Mariner, Pioneer, Viking, Voyager, and Galileo missions.

Sagan helped solve a number of planetary mysteries. One was why Venus is the hottest planet in the solar system. Sagan showed how a thick atmosphere could, like the glass in a greenhouse, prevent solar radiation from leaving the planet. Sagan's idea of a "runaway greenhouse effect" on Venus has helped scientists understand why our own planet's temperature is on the rise from global warming.

Carl Sagan became famous in the 1980s when he narrated a television series based on his book *Cosmos*. Sagan died while *Mars Pathfinder* was heading to Mars. To honor him, NASA renamed its lander the *Carl Sagan Memorial Mars Station*.

The *Viking 2* lander's view of Utopia Planitia on Mars (right); also covered in water-based ice frost (left).

there's water. But the region visited by the Viking spacecraft seemed quite lifeless.

Although it didn't lead to the discovery of extraterrestrial life, the Viking mission was a big success. The orbiters were only designed to last a few months. *Viking 2*'s lasted nearly two years, and *Viking 1*'s orbited for four years until it ran out of fuel. The landers also kept on going and going: the *Viking 1* lander finally fell silent in 1983. The images and information sent back to Earth from the Viking landers and orbiters gave scientists many years of study material and taught us a lot about Mars. Some of the Viking information created more questions than answers. Mars was once a very different place than it is now. It was at one time a planet with water and erupting volcanoes; a planet not that different from ancient Earth. Why did the two planets change into such different worlds? What happened on Mars? And did life ever exist there? It would be 20 years before another spacecraft tried to solve Mars's mysteries.

Parachuting Eggs

activity

Landers like the Viking probes must be able to safely set down on a planet—not crash-land! Space probes bound for a planet's surface have to slow down from space speed to landing speed. A parachute, which opens after the probe enters the planet's atmosphere, does the trick, thanks to air friction acting against the downward pull of gravity. Find out which material makes a better parachute in this activity.

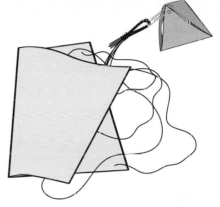

YOU'LL NEED

Ruler

Pencil

8½" x 8½" (22-cm by 22-cm) or larger piece of lightweight cardboard (such as from a large cereal box)

Scissors

Hole punch

3 raw eggs

2 large paper clips

4 36" (1-m) lengths of string

12" x 12" (30-cm x 30-cm) piece of newspaper

12" x 12" (30-cm x 30-cm) piece of cloth

12" x 12" (30-cm x 30-cm) piece of plastic wrap

Packing tape

Stopwatch or clock with a second hand

1. Use a ruler to draw a triangle with three equal sides on the cardboard. Each side needs to be eight and a half (22 cm) inches long. Cut out the triangle.

2. Take one of the triangle corners and fold it over so that its point is at the middle of the triangle's opposite side, as shown. Crease the fold well, then unfold it. Repeat this step with the two remaining corners.

3. Use the hole punch to create one hole near the tip of each point. This is your lander!

4. Load up your lander with its payload—one egg. Once the egg is inside, thread one paper clip through the three punched holes, as shown.

5. Gather together the four lengths of string. Tie a loop in the gathered strings and hook the other large paper clip onto that loop, as shown.

6. The pieces of newspaper, cloth, and plastic wrap are your test parachutes. Pick one to use for your first test. Being careful not to tangle up the strings, tape the free ends of each string to one corner of your first test parachute. Then hook together the lander's paper clip and the paperclip on the end of the parachute's strings. It's done!

7. Find a high place, such as a stairwell, a balcony, or the edge of a deck, to use as a testing ground. Toss the lander and time how long it takes to reach the ground. Did the egg payload survive?

8. Repeat steps six and seven with the other parachutes, replacing any broken eggs. Which material slowed down the lander the most?

How a Gravity Assist Works

How can the gravitational pull of a planet help a spacecraft? It all depends on the spacecraft's aim. If a probe is aimed directly at Venus, for instance, it will crash-land (A). If a speeding probe is aimed to pass very close to Venus, it will be captured in the planet's orbit (B). But what if the probe is aimed to fly closely by Venus, but not too near it? The probe will first be pulled in by Venus's gravity, which speeds it up. But if the probe keeps aiming away

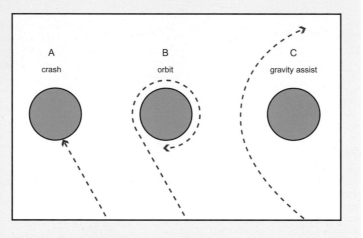

from Venus, it'll swerve and be flung away—with an added boost of speed (C). The extra speed is gained because, as the spacecraft swerves, it is now being dragged through space along the planet's speedy orbit around the Sun. The spacecraft piggybacks a free ride! Venus travels around the Sun at about 78,000 miles per hour (126,000 kph). So a spacecraft moving in the same direction as Venus—rather than straight at it—can catch a real speed boost from a Venus gravity assist—and it's free!

Mariner 10's pictures of Mercury were the first ever taken by a spacecraft. They show moon-like world covered in craters.

SWINGING AROUND MERCURY

The four "inner planets" are Mars, Earth, Venus, and Mercury. NASA checked off the last unvisited, terrestrial, inner planet of the solar system from its list by sending the final Mariner space probe to Mercury. *Mariner 10* was the last in the Mariner series, but it racked up five space firsts! The little space probe was the first (and as yet the only) spacecraft to visit Mercury; the first to explore two planets (Venus and Mercury); the first to revisit a target (Mercury); the first to use the solar winds to orient itself; and the first to use a gravity assist to change its flight path.

Scientists originally planned to have *Mariner 10* fly by Venus and use its gravitational pull on the spacecraft to bend the probe's flight path and give it a fuel-saving fling toward Mercury. This helpful fling is called a gravity assist. The use of gravity assists to speed up spacecraft, save fuel, and cut down on travel time made the dream of sending spacecraft to the outer planets—and beyond—a reality.

Because it's so close to the Sun, Mercury is a hard place to get to. The Sun's heat and gravity

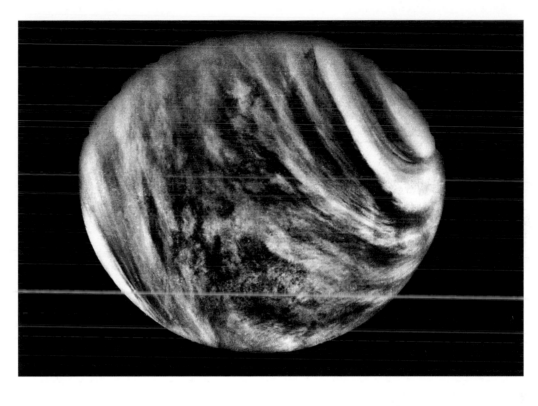

can be overpowering so near it. And adding the tricky gravity assist maneuver for the first time seemed like enough of a challenge to the *Mariner 10* team. But a meeting at NASA's Jet Propulsion Laboratory in 1970 raised the bar. A math professor from the very same college where Galileo Galilei once taught came up

Mariner 10 took this picture of Venus in 1974 as it grabbed a gravity assist that flung it on toward Mercury.

Giuseppe "Bepi" Colombo (1920–1984)

Giuseppe Colombo was a professor at the University of Padua in Italy, where Galileo Galilei once taught. Colombo studied Galileo's life and helped convince the Catholic Church to exonerate Galileo. Colombo, a gifted mathematician, studied the ways planets and suns spin and orbit. Besides teaching and doing research, he worked as an advisor on several NASA and European Space Agency (ESA) missions. In addition to suggesting how *Mariner 10* could make additional flybys of Mercury, Colombo worked on the Jupiter orbiter *Galileo* and the ESA's *Giotto* mission to Halley's comet. Because Colombo's calculations allowed *Mariner 10* to visit Mercury multiple times, the ESA has named its own future Mercury-mapping spacecraft *Bepi-Colombo*. Colombo also thought up the idea of using a long tether to support a spacecraft from an orbiting platform. It resulted in the Tethered Satellite System (TSS) that was launched in 1992 and 1996 aboard the space shuttle.

with another idea. Giuseppe Colombo was a mathematician who studied the formulas and equations that governed the orbits and rotations of planets. Colombo had noticed that, once *Mariner 10* left Mercury and orbited the Sun, that orbit would be about equal to twice Mercury's rotation. The Italian professor suggested that NASA could use that fact to bring *Mariner 10* back to Mercury for a second flyby. The engineers at the meeting didn't really think it was possible. But they looked into it. And they discovered that, by carefully choosing the first flyby point, they could use a gravity assist to swing *Mariner 10* back by Mercury six months later—twice!

Mariner 10 launched in November 1973. It flew by Venus in February 1974, analyzing the atmosphere and snapping thousands of stunning, close-up pictures of swirling clouds. Using a gravity assist from Venus, *Mariner 10* then shot toward Mercury. It got there in only six weeks. In March 1974 *Mariner 10* made its first flyby of Mercury, then looped around the Sun and made another Mercury flyby six months later. After that it went around the Sun again

and came back for a third and final Mercury flyby. To save enough fuel to make the extra flybys, instead of using its thruster engines, *Mariner 10*'s solar panels were used as sails to make course corrections. *Fantastico!*

Most of what we know about Mercury, we know from *Mariner 10*. It's a hard place to see with a telescope because of the Sun's glare. *Mariner 10* sent back images of a gray, cratered, moon-like surface. But surprisingly, Mercury has a very strong magnetic field, which is odd for such a small, slow-spinning planet (one rotation, or day, on Mercury equals 59 Earth days). Scientists think it's probably because Mercury has a giant iron center.

During the 1970s scientists were getting a look at Earth's past—and possible future—by studying the planets with solid land, called terrestrial planets. Mercury and the Moon hold clues to what the solar system was like before millions of years of weather and shifting continents erased the evidence of asteroid impacts on Earth. The atmosphere and conditions on Venus hold lessons for a possible future Earth if global warming trends continue. Perhaps the answer that Carl Sagan wrote in response to the question, "Why explore space?" says it best: "There is a very practical reason as well: We can take better care of Earth (and its inhabitants) by studying it from space and by comparing it with other worlds."

GLIMPSING THE GAS GIANTS

It's difficult to compare Earth to the very different worlds of Jupiter and Saturn. These two planets aren't terrestrial, they are gas giants— worlds of spinning gases and liquids under high pressure. They're also very far away. Jupiter is eight times as far from Earth as Mars is. The distance alone would make getting to Jupiter difficult. To make it even more challenging, Mars and Jupiter are divided by a belt of asteroids— some of them as big as Alaska. Some scientists doubted that a small space probe could make it all the way to Jupiter and Saturn. How could it survive a trip through the asteroid belt? Pioneer was the mission chosen to find out. The two twin flyby space probes, *Pioneer 10* and *Pioneer 11*, were outfitted with cameras and science instruments, and they were the first space

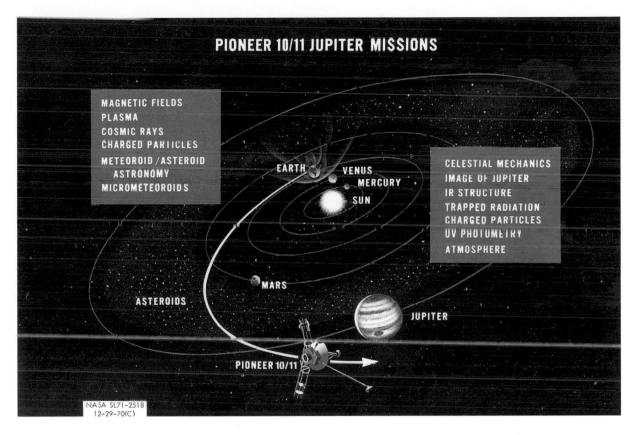

probes powered by nuclear power. The amount of regular fuel needed to travel that far couldn't be carried by a probe, and the sunlight that reaches Jupiter is too faint for solar panels to work.

Pioneer 10 left Earth in March 1972 and safely passed through the asteroid belt in July. It took nearly another year and a half to travel to Jupiter. But it made it, surviving the giant

planet's massive radiation and sending back the first close-up pictures of Jupiter. The probe's twin, *Pioneer 11*, arrived at Jupiter a year later, then traveled on and flew by Saturn in 1979. The Pioneer probe images were fuzzy, but they were just simple spacecraft. They didn't have the onboard computers that the Mariners did. Every command had to be sent directly from someone at NASA on Earth. It took 16,000 commands by mission controllers to get *Pioneer 10* past Jupiter. That's a whole bunch of opportunities to make a mistake! But the Pioneer probes truly lived up to their name. They were the first spacecraft to visit the outer planets. Their extremely successful successors, the Voyager probes (see page 81), would soon follow the trail blazed by the Pioneer missions.

JET-POWERED ASTRONOMY

Astronomers were also trying to get a clearer look at a gas giant planet from Earth. Nearly 200 years after William Herschel had discovered the seventh planet, scientists still didn't know much about Uranus. It was too far away for telescopes to get a very good look at it. And no space probes had visited it. But astronomer James Elliot thought he'd get a special chance to look at Uranus in 1977. Elliot knew that in March 1977 Uranus would pass in front of a star known as SAO 158687 as the planet moved in its orbit. Astronomers often use these kinds of events, called occultations, to find out more about the planets. Astronomers around the world

The Pioneer probes were the first spacecraft to visit the outer planets. Top: *Pioneer 10* took this photograph of Jupiter in 1973. Bottom: *Pioneer 11* encountered and photographed Saturn in 1979.

pointed their telescopes at Uranus and waited for it to pass in front of the star and become backlit. They got ready to measure the amount of and change in the starlight as it passed through Uranus's atmosphere. Elliot's astronomy team wanted to use these measurements to calculate the temperature of Uranus's atmosphere.

The best spot on Earth for viewing the occultation was in the middle of the Indian Ocean. Not a great place to build an observatory! But Elliot and his team had use of NASA's very special observatory—one that could fly. The Kuiper Airborne Observatory (KAO) is a C-141 cargo jet that holds a 36 inch (90 cm) telescope and all kinds of other astronomy instruments. It's a flying observatory. Not only could the KAO go wherever the best view was, but it flew about seven miles (12 km) above the Earth. That put it above most of the clouds and air that blur the view from a telescope on the ground.

On the night of March 10, 1977, the KAO lifted off from a runaway in Australia and headed for the Indian Ocean. Aboard were five crew members and fourteen passengers, including astronomer James Elliot and his team. KAO and

its astronomers got into position and waited for Uranus to pass in front of the star. Then it happened. Just before Uranus was due to pass in front of the star, the amount of starlight suddenly dropped off, then came back up again in an instant. What was that? everyone asked. Then it happened again, and again—five times in total. They were rings! Uranus's never-before-seen rings were blocking the star's light as they passed in front of it.

The astronomers waited for Uranus to complete its pass in front of the star. They wanted to see if the same five dips in starlight happened as the other side of the planet passed in front of the star. Sure enough, as Uranus completed its pass, the amount of starlight dipped five times again. "They're real," said Elliot. Now scientists knew that Saturn was not the only planet to have rings. Five months later *Voyager 2* was launched (see page 81). After a long nine-year journey, *Voyager 2* would get a first-hand look—and take pictures—of the rings that were discovered nearly a decade earlier. James Elliot made sure he was at NASA's Mission Control when the Voyager pictures finally came in.

Gerard Peter Kuiper
(1905–1973)

The Kuiper Airborne Observatory (KAO) was named after astronomer Gerard Peter Kuiper, the father of modern planetary science. He discovered Miranda, the fifth moon around Uranus, and Nereid, the second moon of Neptune.

Kuiper pioneered many techniques in astronomical spectroscopy, the study of light coming from the planets. By observing the kinds of light coming from the planets, Kuiper made many important discoveries and predictions that were later confirmed by space probes. He discovered the methane atmosphere around Saturn's moon Titan and Mars's carbon dioxide atmosphere and water ice polar caps. Even Kuiper's prediction that walking on the Moon would be like walking on crunchy snow was confirmed by Neil Armstrong!

Kuiper predicted that there was a belt of comets and debris past Neptune, also orbiting the Sun. The belt was found in the 1990s and named the Kuiper belt.

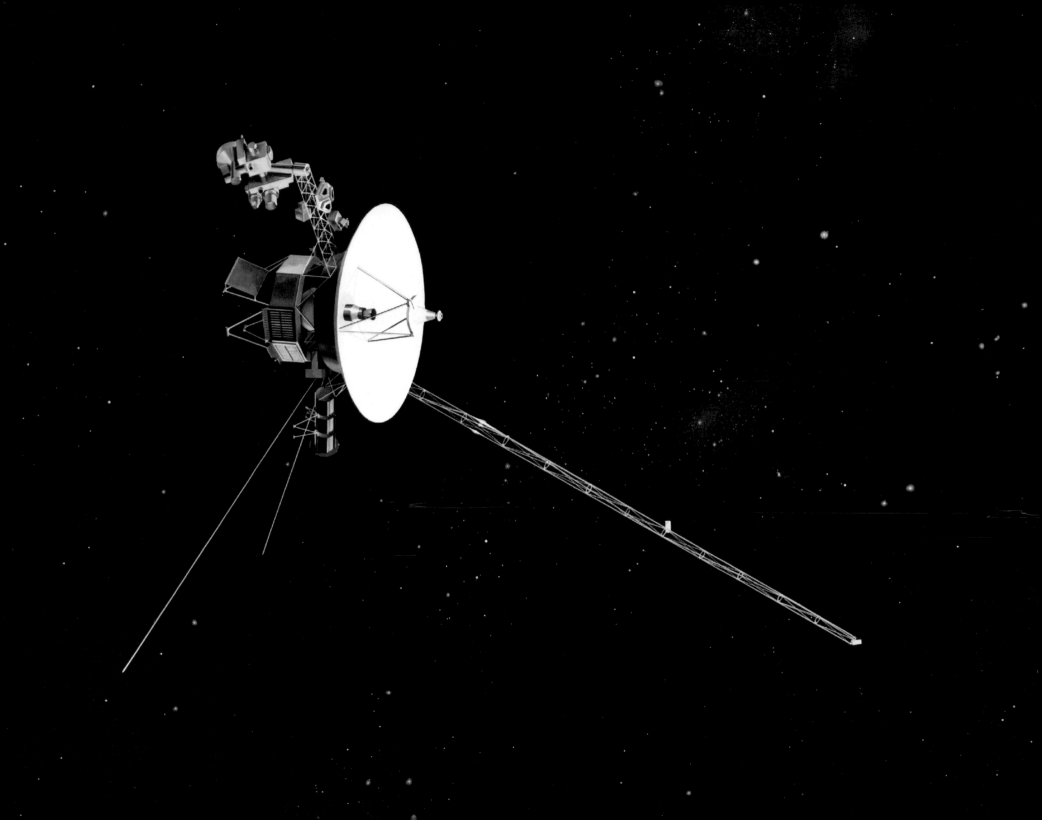

1980s: Voyage to the Outer Planets

5

Once every couple of centuries, something special happens in the outer solar system. About every 175 years the orbits of the four gas giant planets bring them all to the same side of the Sun at the same time. Jupiter, Saturn, Uranus, and Neptune become closer neighbors. NASA scientists figured out that this rare alignment of the outer planets could allow a single space probe to visit all four planets if it was launched in 1977. The next such launch opportunity wouldn't come around again until 2150! Reasoning that two probes had a better chance of success than one, NASA built two spacecraft and launched them at the end of the summer of 1977. *Voyager 1* and *Voyager 2* were on their way to a very special meeting.

THE VOYAGERS

The Voyagers weren't the first to head for the outer solar system. *Pioneer 10* and *Pioneer 11* got there first. *Pioneer 10* flew past Jupiter in 1973, then grabbed enough of a gravity assist from the giant planet to hurl itself on a path that would eventually take it out of the solar system. *Pioneer 11*

Voyager probes the outer solar system.

flew by Jupiter in 1974 and used its gravity-assist maneuver to sling itself toward Saturn. The Pioneer spacecraft were sort of guinea-pig probes. These simple robot explorers proved that spacecraft could safely make it through an asteroid belt, reach the outer planets, and successfully use gravity assists to maneuver. No one knew how much radiation Jupiter put out until *Pioneer 11* was nearly fried with a dose that was 100 times the amount that would kill a person. Everything that was learned from Pioneer helped make the Voyager probes better and their journeys safer and more successful. Thanks, *Pioneer 10* and *Pioneer 11*!

The Voyagers were the best of the bunch of space probes sent out into the solar system during the 1970s. After witnessing the Pioneers' run-in with radiation, NASA added extra protection to the Voyager space probes. Each 1,800-pound (825-kg) Voyager was built for long distances. Jupiter is far from the Sun—five times farther from it than Earth is. Only one-twenty-fifth of the amount of sunlight that hits Earth reaches Jupiter. Solar panels might have been able to supply power to the Mariner and Viking probes, but they wouldn't work for the Voyager mission. Scientists had to come up with different sources of power. They created three small, nuclear-powered generators to create the electricity that runs the Voyager radio receivers, science instruments, and computers. The spacecraft itself gets around with thruster power. These small rockets burn an ammonia-based fuel called hydrazine.

The Voyagers are packed with cameras and science instruments. Their computers make them the smartest space probes ever launched, and they're able to survive on their own far from Earth's engineers. It takes 46 minutes for radio waves from a space probe at Jupiter to reach Earth. That means it takes an hour and a half for a spacecraft at Jupiter to receive and answer a message. The Voyager probes needed to be able to think for themselves, so engineers installed software that allows them to find and correct their own problems. In fact, both *Voyager 1* and *Voyager 2* are now smarter than they were when they left Earth, thanks to the updates and changes to their computers' software sent millions of miles through space. Amazing!

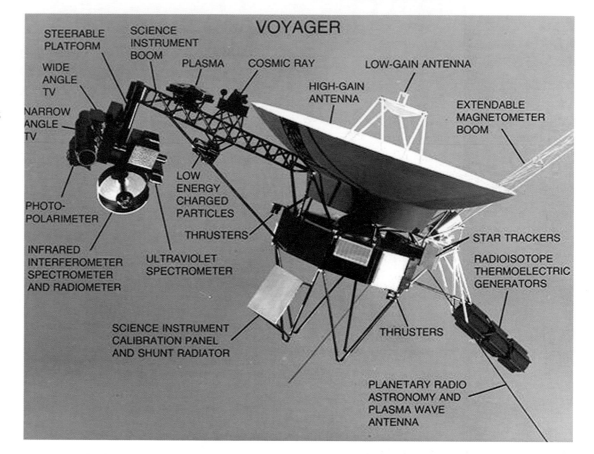

The Voyager probes carry all kinds of scientific instruments. The *Infrared Interferometer Spectrometer* measures infrared radiation given off or reflected by planets or moons, and the *Ultraviolet Spectrometer* does the same for ultraviolet radiation. The *Photopolarimeter* measures the amount of light scattered or reflected from the moons or planets at different wavelengths and angles. The *Cosmic Ray* detector records the number and energy of cosmic ray particles near the spacecraft. The *Low-Energy Charged Particles* detector measures low-energy charged particles trapped in the radiation belts of planets. The *Plasma* detector measures a gas composed of charged particles with very low energies. The *Extendable Magnetometer Boom* measures magnetic fields around planets and moons. The *Planetary Radio Astronomy and Plasma Wave Antennae* detects radio emissions from the planets.

JUPITER AND SATURN

It's a long way to Jupiter. You could fly to Mars eight times and still not quite travel the distance from Earth to Jupiter. But it took the speedy Voyagers only 18 months to get there. What they found on arrival forever changed what we know about the king of planets.

Everyone knows that Jupiter is the biggest planet in the solar system. But it's hard to imagine just how big it is. If you added up the mass of all the other planets in the solar system, the total wouldn't equal Jupiter's mass. In fact, you'd have to double that total to come close! Think of Earth as a small grape. By comparison, Jupiter would be a large grapefruit! In some ways Jupiter is less like a planet and more like a star with its own mini–solar system. Jupiter has dozens of orbiting moons, some of which are larger than Pluto or even Mercury. Each of those moons is very different, as unique as the planets that circle our sun.

The planet Jupiter itself isn't like Earth, Mars, Venus, or Mercury. It's not a terrestrial planet made of solid rock and covered in land. Jupiter— as well as Saturn, Uranus, and Neptune—are gas giants. They're enormous spinning balls of gas and liquid under intense pressure. The worlds of the outer solar system are very different from Earth and its nearby planetary neighbors. And *Voyager 1* and *Voyager 2* had come to find out just how different they are.

First up was Jupiter. The Voyagers immediately detected something amazing. The solar system's biggest planet had a thin ring a little less than 19 miles (30 km) thick! Who knew? The space probes measured Jupiter's gravity fields and temperatures, and they analyzed the chemicals in its thick atmosphere. And what about that great red spot that had puzzled astronomers for centuries? It turned out to be a gigantic storm as big as three Earths!

The Voyagers' discoveries about Jupiter were amazing. But what they found out about Jupiter's moons was even more astonishing.

Voyager 2's view of Jupiter in 1979.

When the Voyagers launched, Jupiter had 13 known moons. *Voyager 1* and *Voyager 2* discovered three more—Thebe, Metis, and Adrastea. When the images of Jupiter's many moons began to arrive back at Earth, everyone was blown away—especially by the moon called Io. This little moon of Jupiter was only half the size of Earth's moon. But it was nothing like any moon ever seen before. Io was yellow, orange, and brown, and it was covered with active volcanoes spewing stuff into space. It was the first time any active volcanoes had ever been seen except on Earth. (Mars's ancient volcanoes are long dead.) The Voyagers also found evidence of a liquid ocean beneath the frozen crust of Jupiter's moon Europa, and plate tectonics on the surface of Ganymede.

Next up was Saturn. *Voyager 1* and *Voyager 2* grabbed a gravity assist from Jupiter and arrived at the sixth planet in 1980 and 1981. The sights at Saturn were just as mind-blowing. The Voyagers found winds in Saturn's clouds with speeds of up to 1,100 miles (1,770 km) per hour—four times a very strong tornado's wind speed. And those rings! Astronomers since

Voyager 2's view of Saturn and four of its icy moons—Tethys, Dione, Rhea, and Mimas. Can you spot them all?

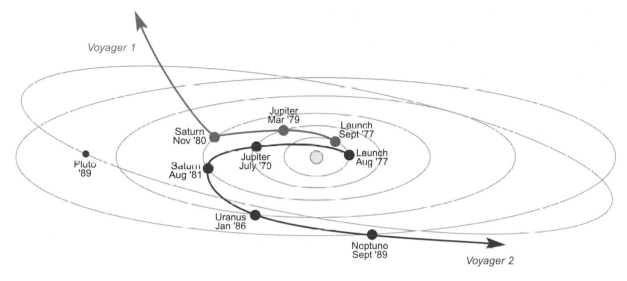

The journeys of *Voyager 1* and *Voyager 2*.

Voyager 1's view of Jupiter's moon Io in 1979 revealed many volcanoes.

Galileo have gazed in wonder at Saturn's shimmering rings. Thanks to the Voyagers, they now know that the rings are actually made up of thousands of ringlets, each its own ever-changing mass of ice, rock, dust, and snow, in every imaginable size and combination. The Voyagers also discovered five new moons to add to the 13 known Saturn moons. *Voyager 1* found a thick nitrogen atmosphere on the moon Titan, not unlike the atmosphere that once surrounded Earth billions of years ago.

Voyager 1 paid a price for getting so close to Titan. It was now flying on a trajectory that led it away from the other planets. Four years into their mission, the Voyagers were splitting up. When NASA launched *Voyager 1* and *Voyager 2*, its primary goal was to visit Jupiter and Saturn. *Voyager 2* was really a backup probe that would be ready to step in for its twin in case of trouble. But both spacecraft were still doing well, and their mission was, so far, a stunning success. So NASA decided to try for an encore.

While *Voyager 1* headed out of the solar system, *Voyager 2* caught a boost from Saturn's gravity and set a course for a planet no spacecraft had ever seen—Uranus. It would take more than four years to get there.

ODD URANUS

Ellis Miner likes to understand how things work. Some of his earliest childhood memories are about trying to figure things out. "For my eighth birthday, my parents gave me an erector set that immediately and forever became my favorite pastime," says Miner. And it was—at least, until a high-school physics course put him on the path to being a scientist. Miner studied physics in college, and he liked astronomy as a hobby. The two interests came together in graduate school around 1962 when "astrophysics and the NASA Space Program became the objects of my affection," Miner explains. He soon began working at NASA's Jet Propulsion Laboratory, and he's been there ever since. "The amazement is in recognizing that, by exploring space, we are doing something that's never been done before—that we are

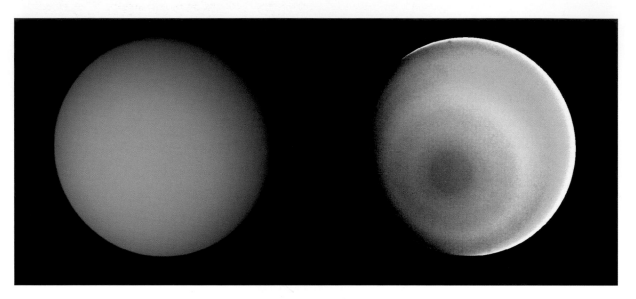

These two images of Uranus were sent back by *Voyager 2* in 1986. The one on the left is in "true color"—it shows what you'd see if you could look right at Uranus from a spacecraft. The image on the right is in "false color"—a combination of images taken through blue, green, and orange filters. The orange area is haze over the pole.

discovering—that there are many interesting things in space," Miner says.

Ellis Miner first worked on the Mariner missions and then on Viking. Next he was hired by NASA to be the Voyager mission's Deputy Project Scientist. The Jupiter and Saturn flybys had been a big success. But Miner and the rest of the Voyager team had their work cut out for them in getting *Voyager 2* ready for Uranus. The space probes had really been designed just to

reach Saturn, after all. And Uranus is a lot farther out. Would NASA be able to send and receive messages to and from *Voyager 2*? To help boost faraway communication, NASA beefed up its information-receiving Deep Space Network (see page 93) antennas. The Australians pitched in two of theirs to help out too.

In addition to being much farther away, Uranus is a lot colder and darker than Saturn. The sunlight that reaches Uranus is four times weaker than the sunlight at Saturn and almost 400 times weaker than the sunlight here on Earth. *Voyager 2* was basically going to have to take pictures in the dark.

Engineers worked on all of these problems. They upgraded *Voyager 2*'s computer software to be able to squeeze more information into every message and transmit pictures more quickly. "*Voyager 2* is now a smarter spacecraft than it was when it went by Saturn, and a lot smarter than when we launched it," Miner told a reporter. But could it make it to the seventh planet?

Eight years after leaving Earth, *Voyager 2* reached Uranus. It made it! NASA's gamble of going for the encore paid off. The miraculous spacecraft passed within 50,000 miles (80,500 km) of the planet's cloud tops. Thanks to *Voyager 2*, we now know that a day on fast-spinning Uranus is only 17 hours long! *Voyager 2* carefully wove through the ring system that had been discovered by James Elliot (see page 79) in 1977, photographing their dust- to boulder-sized particles. The moons again stole the show. *Voyager 2* discovered 10 new moons, bringing Uranus's satellite total to 15. The oddest moon

Know the Code!

activity

The pictures, computer messages, and collected information sent back to Earth from a space probe is digitized—just like a digital camera image, a cell phone call, or a fax. The information is sent in a code made up of only 1s and 0s. This is called binary code. In this activity you can decode binary messages and images, then create some of your own.

YOU'LL NEED

Red pencil or pen

Graph paper

Black or blue pen

Plain lead pencil

1. Using the red pencil or pen, outline a grid on the graph paper that is 10 graph squares wide by 10 graph squares long. Your graph will consist of 100 squares.

2. Using the pen, you will write either a 1 or a 0 in each of the squares. Ready? Here are the numbers by row, starting at the top: Row 1: 0 0 0 0 0 0 0 0 0 0; Row 2: 0 0 1 0 0 1 0 0 0 0; Row 3: 0 0 1 0 0 1 0 1 0 0; Row 4: 0 0 1 0 0 1 0 0 0 0; Row 5: 0 0 1 1 1 1 0 1 0 0; Row 6: 0 0 1 0 0 1 0 1 0 0; Row 7: 0 0 1 0 0 1 0 1 0 0; Row 8: 0 0 1 0 0 1 0 1 0 0; Row 9: 0 0 1 0 0 1 0 1 0 0; Row 10: 0 0 0 0 0 0 0 0 0 0. The finished grid should look like the grid below.

0	0	0	0	0	0	0	0	0	0
0	0	1	0	0	1	0	0	0	0
0	0	1	0	0	1	0	1	0	0
0	0	1	0	0	1	0	0	0	0
0	0	1	1	1	1	0	1	0	0
0	0	1	0	0	1	0	1	0	0
0	0	1	0	0	1	0	1	0	0
0	0	1	0	0	1	0	1	0	0
0	0	1	0	0	1	0	1	0	0
0	0	0	0	0	0	0	0	0	0

3. Now use plain lead pencil to lightly shade in each square that contains a 1. Leave the squares with 0s in them blank. What's the message?

4. Now decode a different kind of message. Repeat step 1 and then fill in the grid with this code: Row 1: 1 0 0 0 0 0 1 0 0 0; Row 2: 0 1 0 0 0 1 0 0 0 0; Row 3: 0 0 1 0 1 0 0 0 0 0; Row 4: 0 1 1 1 1 1 0 0 0 0; Row 5: 0 1 0 1 0 1 0 0 0 1; Row 6: 0 1 1 1 1 1 0 0 1 0; Row 7: 0 1 0 1 0 1 0 1 0 0; Row 8: 0 1 0 0 1 0 1 0 0; Row 9: 0 1 1 1 1 1 0 1 0 0; Row 10: 0 0 1 1 1 0 0 1 0 0. Get the picture?

5. You can make your own binary messages. Just shade in squares on graph paper to create a picture or message. Write in 1s on the shaded squares and 0s on the blank ones. Then write out the rows into strings of 0s and 1s, as shown in steps 2 and 4 above. You can give your binary message to a friend and ask him or her to decode it.

is Miranda, which seems to have a combination of everything—deep canyons, twisted ridges, craters, and totally bizarre, v-shaped gouges called chevrons. "What we have seen thus far has been spectacular," Miner told reporters. Now *Voyager 2* was given a chance for a second encore! The space probe was sent on its way to Neptune, too.

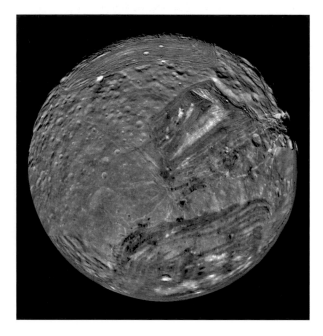

Voyager 2's view of Uranus's rugged moon Miranda in 1986.

NEPTUNE AND BEYOND

More than a dozen years after its launch, *Voyager 2* reached our solar system's farthest planet. Back in 1989 when *Voyager 2* arrived at Neptune, Pluto was still called the ninth planet. But even so, Neptune was farther from the Sun during *Voyager 2*'s visit. Pluto orbits along a different plane than all the other planets. (See the Voyager diagram on page 85.) Pluto's odd slanted orbit takes it inside Neptune's path for 20 years of its 248-year orbit. Arriving while Pluto was inside Neptune's orbit meant that *Voyager 2* had not only traveled three times farther and eight years longer than it was designed to. It had also made it out past Pluto!

Voyager 2 made the most of its trip to Neptune. It maneuvered a close-up flyby within 3,000 miles (4,800 km) of Neptune's north pole. It discovered that, like the rest of its gas giant cousins, Neptune has a ring system. It also discovered six new moons. *Voyager 2* measured winds on Neptune that were nearly as fast as Saturn's, and it detected clouds made

This picture shows *Voyager 2*'s view of blue Neptune as it would appear when viewed near Triton, its largest moon.

of methane. *Voyager 2* also snapped photos of a huge storm the size of Earth in Neptune's Southern Hemisphere. But Ellis Miner told reporters, "In terms of mission highlights, Triton is the most interesting."

Triton is Neptune's largest moon and one of the oddest in the solar system. Triton has a retrograde orbit—it travels around the Sun in the opposite direction that Neptune does! Its temperature is about -391°F (-199°C), making it the coldest known place in the solar system. Its surface is odd, too. One side of Triton looks like pebbly cantaloupe skin, and the other is extremely rugged. *Voyager 2* even captured bizarre images of geysers spewing out nitrogen gas on Triton.

Once past Neptune, *Voyager 2* headed out of the solar system—just as *Voyager 1* had done before it. But the Voyagers' mission isn't finished. After more than 10,000 days of operation, both space probes have seven science instruments still working. They'll continue to send back information about what's past the planets until 2020 by measuring solar wind, cosmic rays, and plasma waves. Even after we lose contact with

them, *Voyager 1* and *Voyager 2* will keep moving through space. They could easily survive for thousands of years. Just in case another form of life finds them someday, both Voyagers carry a greeting. A disc of sounds and images from Earth is attached to each space probe.

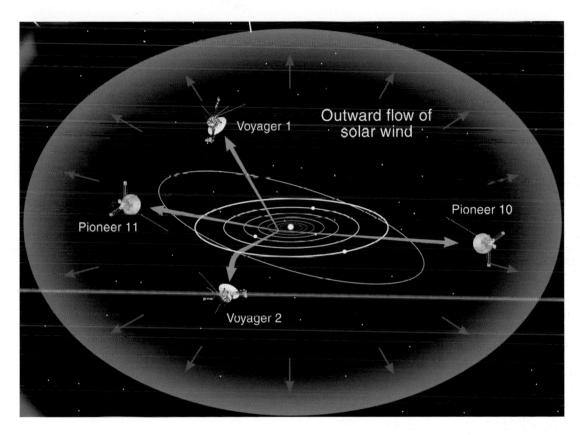

Voyagers 1 and 2 and Pioneers 10 and 11 are on their way out of the solar system.

Greetings from Earth

Four NASA spacecraft are now on their way out of the solar system and bound for interstellar space. *Voyager*s *1* and *2* and *Pioneer*s *10* and *11* were sent to explore the outer reaches of our solar system, but they are now headed beyond it. When they were launched in the 1970s, scientists knew the probes might go where no probe had gone before. Just in case someone from another solar system were to find one of the Pioneer probes someday, both were outfitted with a plaque describing the spacecraft, human beings, and the location of our solar system. The Voyager probes each carry a gold disc. The disk is a greeting to the universe and has recorded sounds, pictures, and messages from Earth.

If you were in charge of creating the next greeting from Earth to travel on a space probe, what messages, sounds, pictures, and information would you include? A map to Earth? Information about the humans

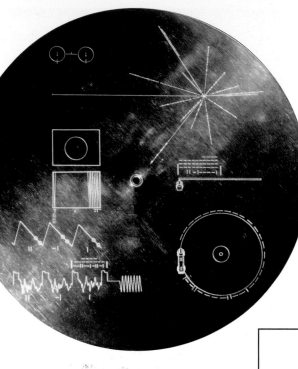

Above: The golden disc found on the Voyager probes. Right: The plaque aboard both Pioneer spacecraft.

who live here? A description of what our world looks like? An invitation to visit? Put together your own "Greetings from Earth" message. Gather up pictures, recordings, facts, and messages that you think would tell aliens about us. You can put the pictures into a folder, include written messages, and add an audio-tape or videotape of songs or spoken messages. If you have a computer, consider putting all the images, songs, and messages onto a CD or a DVD.

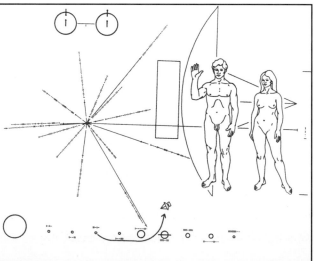

Voyager was the most successful interplanetary mission ever. It visited four planets and discovered 48 moons and dozens of rings. "Voyager was probably the most exciting project I've worked on at JPL," Miner said. "I doubt very much that there will ever be a mission as great as Voyager." Its greatness lies in more than just the sum of all its discoveries. The worlds it explored showed a solar system that is much more varied than anyone had thought. Many of the moons of the gas giants were discovered to be alive with active volcanoes, moving plates, and even geysers. Many scientists believe that the best chance of finding life in the solar system is on one of the moons first photographed by a Voyager.

A COMET RETURNS

Astronomer Edmond Halley's good friend Isaac Newton had solved the mystery of why the planets orbit the Sun. People finally had a name for the force that governed the movement of the planets—gravity. Halley remembered his conversations with Newton while he was studying comets in the late 1600s. Halley was calculating the orbits of different comets seen throughout history when he noticed something extraordinary. The orbit of a comet seen in 1531 and that of another seen in 1607 were nearly the same. And their orbits looked very much like that of a comet Halley had himself observed in 1682. Could these actually all be the very same comet, traveling on a regular path within our solar system—just like a planet?

Most people before Halley's time didn't believe that comets had regular orbits, or that they were even part of the solar system. Humans had observed comets for thousands of years. Those who were superstitious saw comets as meddlesome heavenly visitors, and they blamed famines, drought, and wars on the comets' unannounced appearances. But Halley knew better. In 1705 he published the book *A Synopsis of the Astronomy of Comets*. In it Halley described the orbits of the comets seen in 1531, 1607, and 1682. Halley argued that they were in fact the orbits of the very same comet, and he predicted that the comet's orbit would bring it back by Earth in 1758. On Christmas Day of that very year the comet

Edmond Halley (1656–1742)

Edmond Halley went to study at Oxford University in England at age 17. He visited the Royal Greenwich Observatory and luckily met the royal astronomer of the time, John Flamsteed. Halley was soon studying astronomy.

Flamsteed had used the observatory's telescope to create a catalog of all the stars that were visible from the Northern Hemisphere. Halley decided to follow in the royal astronomer's footsteps and do the same for the Southern Hemisphere. At age 20 Halley set sail for an island in the southern Atlantic Ocean. Within a year he'd recorded the positions of 341 stars. His southern star catalog, published in 1678, made him a well-known astronomer.

Halley made one of his biggest contributions to science when he helped publish his friend Isaac Newton's discovery of gravity in *Principia Mathematica*. Edmond Halley became England's Royal Astronomer in 1720 and served in the position until his death.

International Halley Watch organized 800 scientists from 40 countries, making sure that all of the big observatories were aiming their telescopes at Halley's comet and capturing pictures like this one, on March 8, 1986.

was sighted. From then on it was called Halley's comet in the astronomer's honor.

As it turned out, observations of Halley's comet go back to 240 B.C., when Chinese astronomers recorded observations of it. It's been seen about every 76 years since. There are many comets that have orbits that bring them through our solar system. But none passes by so often and so brightly that it can be seen with the naked eye. Halley's comet may be the world's most famous comet. But besides its 76-year orbit, not much was known about it before

the space age. Space probes were going to change that. Everyone knew that Halley's comet would be back in 1986. Three nations readied five spacecraft to fly out and greet it.

RENDEZVOUS WITH HALLEY

Halley's comet welcomed many visitors in March 1986. The first to arrive were *Vega 1* and *Vega 2*. The two Soviet spacecraft had been launched toward Venus in late 1984. Once there, the Vegas released landers that studied the soil and air of our sister planet. Then the spacecraft

grabbed a push from Venus's gravity to head for Halley's comet. The five-ton Soviet probes flew within 4,971 miles (8,000 km) of the famous comet on March 6 and 9, 1986. They snapped hundreds of pictures of the thick dust around the comet's solid center with its jets of bright gas gushing out. Meanwhile, two Japanese probes began studying Halley from a safer distance. *Sakigake* and *Suisei* studied the comet's tail of gas and dust with an ultraviolet imager. The small spacecraft also gathered information about the solar wind around the comet.

Thanks to navigation information collected by the Vegas, the most sophisticated comet visitor would be able to get the closest. *Giotto* was the European Space Agency's very first interplanetary mission. The space probe was well outfitted for an encounter with a dust- and gas-gushing comet. It had a two-tiered protective shield and a solid, compact, drum-like shape. *Giotto* would depend on this protection for its survival.

On March 14, 1986, *Giotto* approached Halley from a distance of 376 miles (605 km). Dust bits hit the speeding space probe about 100

Keeping in Touch

Sending spacecraft to analyze rocks on Mars, measure winds on Neptune, and snap photos of Halley's comet doesn't accomplish much if the images and information don't make it back to Earth. That's where NASA's Deep Space Network steps in. The DSN is an international network of antennae that receives and sends messages, images, and information back and forth between interplanetary spacecraft and NASA.

The DSN has been around since the late 1950s, when NASA started launching satellites. As spacecraft traveled farther and became more sophisticated, the DSN improved and grew. More and better antennae were added to the global network to receive radio transmissions from *Voyager 2*, for instance. And the technology that transmits the data became faster and better, too. In 1965 data from *Mariner 9* at Mars came in at eight bits per second. By 1979 it was being received from Voyager at Jupiter at 116,000 bits per second. A network of antennae around the world is required for sending spacecraft into the outer solar system. One reason that the Soviet Union didn't attempt missions past Mars was that it didn't have a network of antennae outside the USSR.

Today, three separate sites equally spaced across Earth make up the DSN. The three DSN sites are in California's Mojave Desert; near Madrid, Spain; and outside Canberra, Australia. Their spread-out placement means that at least one can be in contact with spacecraft at all times as the Earth rotates. The DSN's high-tech, steerable, high-gain parabolic reflector antennae make the DSN the largest and most sensitive scientific tele-communications system in the world.

These three 110-foot (34-m) antennae in the Mojave Desert are part of the Deep Space Network.

times per second, caking up a layer of at least 57 pounds (26 kg) of dust. The dust was so thick that it knocked *Giotto*'s antenna out of alignment, causing it to lose contact with Earth. But data started coming back in after a very long 32 minutes. *Giotto* had survived its visit to Halley! And it sent back 2,000 photographs, along with measurements of the comet's water, gas, and chemical makeup.

Giotto and the other Halley-visiting spacecraft made many discoveries about comets. A comet is a sort of dirty snowball flying through space. Halley was clocked at 80,000 miles (128,000 km) per hour! Its core, or nucleus, is a ball consisting of about half ice and half rocky dust. Halley's solid nucleus turned out to be a potato-shaped oval about 9 by 5 miles (15 by 8 km) in size. Like most comets, Halley's nucleus is about 80 percent water-based ice and 15 percent frozen carbon monoxide, and the rest is a mix of frozen carbon dioxide, methane, and ammonia.

Scientists were surprised, however, to find a dark black crust of dust and rock covering most of the ice in Halley's nucleus. As Halley nears the Sun, its heat vaporizes some of the ice that

The European Space Agency readies its comet-chasing spacecraft *Giotto* for launch in 1985.

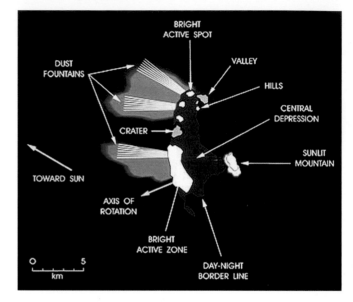

The *Giotto* space probe identified many interesting features found on Halley's comet.

is exposed by holes in the crust covering the nucleus. Bright jets of gas and dust erupt out of the holes and stream out into a glowing tail that's millions of miles long. Every time Halley passes by the Sun it gets a little smaller, as millions of tons of its icy nucleus evaporate. Scientists estimate that Halley's comet will last about another thousand trips past the Sun—and the Earth. Make sure you look for it in 2061!

Kitchen Comet Nucleus

activity

Comets are dirty snowballs with long glowing tails that orbit the Sun. While comets may be from outer space, their ingredients are common on Earth. You can make something very similar to the solid center, or nucleus, of a comet with household ingredients and dry ice. (CAUTION: Dry ice is so cold that it will cause frost burn. Only handle dry ice while wearing protective gloves.)

Adult supervision required

YOU'LL NEED

2–3 pounds of dry ice (available at many ice companies, party stores, and ice cream parlors)

Freezer or cooler filled with water-ice

3 plastic trash bags

Insulated waterproof gloves (or warm gloves covered with plastic dishwashing gloves)

Old towel

Hammer or mallet

Large plastic mixing bowl

2 cups water

2 tablespoons dirt

Ammonia-based window or floor cleaner

2 tablespoons syrup, honey, or molasses

Large mixing spoon

1- or 2-cup measuring cup

Shallow pan or dish

Hair dryer (optional)

1. Keep the dry ice well wrapped and in a freezer or cooler filled with water-ice. It will start to disappear (sublimate) immediately!
2. Make a two-layered bag with two of the trash bags.
3. Put on the gloves. Move the dry ice into the doubled bag. Twist the bag closed, fold it over, and set it back into the cooler. Cover the bag with an old towel. Use the hammer or mallet to crush the dry ice inside the bag. Pound the ice until you have at least two cups of well-crushed dry ice—not chunks.
4. Use the third trash bag to line the mixing bowl.
5. Mix the ingredients of a comet in the bowl. Pour the water into the mixing bowl. Then add the dirt, a couple of sprays or drops of ammonia-based cleaner, and the organic compounds (syrup, honey, or molasses). Stir until well mixed.

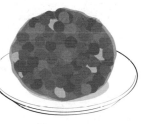

6. Wearing the gloves, mix in 2 cups of crushed dry ice while stirring. It will be a slushy comet at first. But keep stirring until it's nearly frozen solid.
7. Lift the trash bag liner and frozen mix out of the bowl. Wrap the trash bag around the mix, using your gloved hands to shape the comet like a snowball through the bag until it holds its shape.

8. Take the finished comet nucleus out of the bag and set it into a shallow pan or dish where you can watch it melt without it making a mess. The water-based ice will melt into liquid. But the carbon dioxide ice will change, or sublimate, from ice to gas. This is exactly what comets do when they're heated by the Sun. Also watch for small jets of carbon dioxide escaping through holes in the frozen water coating—just like on a real comet! You can also simulate a comet's tail by using a hairdryer set on low to create the "solar wind."

The *Hubble Space Telescope* being repaired and serviced by space shuttle astronaut F. Story Musgrave (top) and astronaut-astronomer Jeffrey Hoffman (bottom) in 1993.

1990s: A Telescope in Space and a Rover on Mars

6

Between 1979 and 1989, NASA didn't launch a single spacecraft to explore the planets. But the 1990s would see a revival of planetary space-probe launches and the beginning of a new age in solar system exploration. It was a new era for many reasons. Whatever Cold War space-race competition lingered during the 1980s further faded when the Union of Soviet Socialist Republics fell apart in 1991. The former Soviet space program became the Russian Space Agency, which concentrates mainly on human space-flight missions, such as space stations. Exploration of other planets was left mostly to the United States and a growing number of other nations and space agencies. International cooperation in space exploration has become the rule, not the exception. The greatest example of that is the International Space Station. By the end of the 1990s, 15 nations would join together to begin assembling the first permanent, crewed, orbiting outpost.

The ways in which space was explored changed in this new era, as did the nationalities of those who explored the solar system. Smaller budgets for solar system exploration created a call for "smaller, cheaper, faster" space-probe programs at NASA. By then, fortunately, engineers and scientists had the basics worked out. They knew what it took to get a robotic spacecraft to another planet in one piece. NASA wanted project leaders to come up with cheaper versions of probes that had already been successful. Because they didn't have to start from scratch on each project, this would cut down on the time and money needed to go from idea to launch.

A NEW VIEW FROM SPACE

What was NASA launching all those years during the 1980s when they weren't sending out planetary probes? A reusable, crewed spacecraft that launches like a rocket, orbits Earth, and later lands like an airplane—the space shuttle. While the space shuttle was primarily designed with human spaceflight in mind, it turned out to work as a new kind of launch vehicle, too. Instead of being sent into space on top of a rocket, satellites and space probes could be carried to space inside the space shuttle, then sent on their way from Earth's orbit. A number of space probes have been launched from the bays

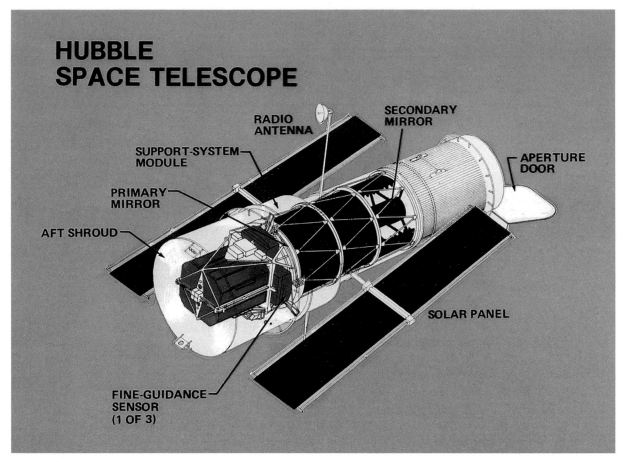

HUBBLE SPACE TELESCOPE

RADIO ANTENNA

SECONDARY MIRROR

SUPPORT-SYSTEM MODULE

APERTURE DOOR

PRIMARY MIRROR

AFT SHROUD

SOLAR PANEL

FINE-GUIDANCE SENSOR (1 OF 3)

How does the *Hubble Space Telescope* work? Its *aperture door* opens to let in light from a planet or star. That light hits the 8-foot (2.5-m) *primary mirror*, bounces off it, and hits the smaller *secondary mirror*. From there the light is reflected into the brownish box of cameras and other instruments behind the *aft shroud*.

The *Hubble Space Telescope* isn't just a telescope—it's also a spacecraft. It zooms through space, circling the Earth every 97 minutes. It's powered by *solar panels*, points itself toward what it wants to see with the help of *fine-guidance sensors*, and uses its *radio antenna* to send back pictures and receive commands.

of the space shuttles, including *Galileo, Magellan,* and *Ulysses.* But the most valuable tool of solar system exploration ever put into space by the space shuttle is the *Hubble Space Telescope.*

Why haul a giant, 11-ton (10,000-kg) telescope the size of a school bus all the way to space? To get a better view. Earth's atmosphere makes a mess for astronomers on Earth. All that thick, moving air causes the light reflected off planets to jiggle and blur when seen through Earth-based telescopes. (It's also what makes stars twinkle.) Planets don't twinkle like stars because they're so much closer to us. Many observatories are situated on top of mountains or in the dry desert to cut down on the atmospheric particles that cause blurring. But even those places can still get blurred views. The *Hubble Space Telescope* orbits about 380 miles (610 km) above Earth, beyond the foggy atmosphere. The view is so much better up there that the telescope could clearly show the fine print on a newspaper from a mile away.

The *Hubble Space Telescope* was put into orbit in 1990 by the space shuttle *Discovery.* Its main job has been to "follow in the footsteps" of its namesake Edwin Hubble (see page 102) and study the evolution of the universe by observing distant galaxies, black holes, and star nurseries. But some of the *Hubble*'s most amazing images have come from its own backyard—our solar system. The workhorse space telescope has photographed Mars's seasons, storms on Saturn, and Uranus's clouds. It even gave us our first look at the surface of Pluto in 1996 (see page 130). But something even more dramatic happened in 1994. A comet was headed on a collision course with Jupiter. And, thanks to the *Hubble*, astronomer Heidi Hammel had a front-row seat.

THE GREAT COMET CRASH OF 1994

Heidi Hammel didn't have a telescope as a kid. But she did learn the constellations while looking out the window from the back seat of her parents' car. It was something to do when she felt carsick on long trips! "And then, when I got into college, I took an astronomy course that was just so much fun," said Hammel. Her professor just happened to be James Elliot,

This series of pictures shows the impact and effects, over time, of a chunk of comet Shoemaker-Levy 9 slamming into Jupiter. Look for the plume of white debris shooting up into space in the top image, and the growing dark impact sites in the other images.

the same astronomer who'd discovered rings around Uranus (see page 79). "I loved working with telescopes, I loved taking pictures of things, taking data, and I just stuck with it." Hammel decided to become an astronomer. Many astronomers study stars, galaxies, nebulae, and quasars. But Hammel chose to study things closer to home—the planets. "You feel like you're exploring when you're doing planetary astronomy," Hammel explained. "Maybe you're not physically walking on the surface of the planet, but you are exploring it for the first time. You're the pioneer."

Hammel studies the gas giants of the outer solar system. (Her favorite is Neptune.) She was using the *Hubble Space Telescope* to watch these odd outer worlds when she was put in charge of a team of scientists who planned to focus *Hubble*'s cameras on a comet. The comet, named Shoemaker-Levy 9, was discovered near Jupiter in May 1993. Gravity from the solar system's biggest world had ripped the comet apart. Now it was a chain of 21 comet chunks, hurtling toward Jupiter at 36 miles (58 km) per second. What would happen when each mile-wide comet

Astronomer Heidi Hammel (second from left, pointing to monitor) and other *Hubble* scientists watch the Great Comet Crash of 1994.

chunk hit the planet? Observatories all over the world turned their telescopes toward Jupiter to see the cosmic collision. Hammel's team readied the telescope that would have the clearest view—the orbiting *Hubble*.

July 16, 1994, was the first day of the great comet crash. A giant chunk of comet slammed into Jupiter's upper atmosphere and exploded with the force of a 200,000-megaton nuclear bomb. The plume of gas and debris shot nearly 1,000 miles (1,600 km) out into space. "This is the kind of stuff I've been dreaming about!" exclaimed Hammel as she watched *Hubble*'s images come in. And it was only the first hit. Every eight hours over the next week, another huge chunk of comet smashed into Jupiter.

Each collision left dark splotches twice as wide as Earth. They were so big that even backyard stargazers with amateur telescopes could see where the comet chunks had hit. "This wasn't something just for astronomers," Hammel recalled. "It belonged to everyone."

A CLOSER LOOK AT JUPITER

The *Hubble Space Telescope* wasn't the only space traveler to see comet Shoemaker-Levy 9 slam into Jupiter. A spacecraft launched toward Jupiter nearly five years earlier arrived just in time to watch the big show. NASA's *Galileo* mission had a rough start. The 20-foot-tall (6-m-tall) probe was so massive that no rocket was powerful enough to launch it directly toward Jupiter. It weighed as much as two SUVs! It was decided that the space shuttle would carry *Galileo* into orbit and launch it on a path that flew first by Venus, then looped around Earth twice to get a big enough gravity assist to send it onto Jupiter. But *Galileo*'s launch was delayed a number of years after the space shuttle *Challenger*'s accident in 1986. *Galileo* was finally sent into space on October 18, 1989. After zipping around

Technicians get *Galileo* ready for its launch from the space shuttle in 1989.

Edwin Hubble (1889–1953)

It wasn't until after becoming a lawyer—and hating it—that Edwin Hubble decided to be an astronomer. Hubble began working at the Mt. Wilson Observatory in California in the 1920s. There he studied the hazy patches of the sky called nebulae. At the time, many astronomers believed that everything in the universe was part of our Milky Way galaxy. But Hubble showed that some of those faraway, faint clouds of light were actually different, separate, previously unknown galaxies. The universe suddenly got much bigger! Based on images from the orbiting telescope named in his honor, the *Hubble Space Telescope*, astronomers today estimate that there are about 125 billion galaxies in the universe.

Edwin Hubble's greatest discovery came in 1929. Hubble figured out that the farther a galaxy is from Earth, the faster it appears to move away. The big bang theory is based on Hubble's discovery. The rate at which the universe is expanding is called the Hubble constant.

Venus, the high-gain antenna on the orbiter failed to fully open. That meant that NASA had to rely on *Galileo*'s low-gain antenna, which could only handle about 70 percent of the information collected by the probe.

But *Galileo* soldiered on, making all kinds of amazing discoveries in spite of its problems. After snapping its own pictures of the Great Comet Crash, *Galileo* approached Jupiter, where it released a small atmospheric probe. The small probe parachuted down through the atmosphere for about an hour, recording and sending weather and cloud information. The probe discovered that Jupiter is made up of about the same percentage of helium as the Sun. Once the tub-sized probe hit atmospheric pressures 20 times greater than Earth's and a temperature of 305°F (152°C), it quit transmitting. Eventually Jupiter's high heat and pressure completely vaporized the aluminum-titanium probe.

Meanwhile, *Galileo* went into orbit around Jupiter in 1995. It flew by the giant planet's many moons multiple times as it circled around Jupiter. The spacecraft was only designed to orbit Jupiter for two years. But once there, it

kept going and going! *Galileo* finally began running out of fuel, so NASA's scientists directed it to crash into Jupiter in 2003. No one wanted an out-of-control spacecraft accidentally contaminating one of Jupiter's moons—which may have life. *Galileo* traveled more than 2.8 billion miles (4.6 billion km) during its 14-year mission, surely making up for its "troubled childhood."

JUPITER'S MOONS

Some of the biggest surprises delivered by the orbiter came from the four moons that had first been discovered by the spacecraft's namesake, Galileo Galilei. *Galileo* found a salty ocean up to 62 miles (100 km) deep hiding underneath the frozen surface of Europa. It also found organic compounds—chemicals often associated with life—there. Is there life hiding under Europa's ice? Images from another Jupiter moon, Callisto, showed an ancient cratered world that has not changed in 4 billion years. And *Galileo* found something on Ganymede that no other known moon possesses—a magnetic field. Some of *Galileo*'s most impressive photographs are of Jupiter's fourth moon, Io. The spacecraft's pictures and data of Io showed the moon to be the most volcanically active place in the solar system! Lava and plumes from active volcanoes dotted Io. Scientist Rosaly Lopes had been getting ready to identify and study Io's volcanoes for years. *Galileo* didn't disappoint her.

Studying volcanoes on another world combined both of Lopes's interests—astronomy and volcanoes. She's been an astronomy buff since childhood, and the moon landings made her want to be an astronaut. But she didn't think her chances were very good "being from Brazil and a girl," Lopes remembered. Even though everyone thought she was crazy to study astronomy, she did it anyway. And then she got hooked on volcanoes while on a field trip to volcanic Mt. Etna in Italy. A crater only a mile away exploded while Lopes was there, killing several people. "I really learned to respect volcanoes," Lopes said. Lopes later went to work for NASA as a planetary volcanologist. Her job was to plan *Galileo*'s observations of Io and its volcanoes.

"What I love best is the feeling of exploring space," says Lopes. "I consider myself an explorer, and I love going to new places and finding new

Galileo **and its atmospheric probe studied and photographed Jupiter's clouds. This 3-D image of cloud layers was taken by** *Galileo* **in 1996.**

things—for example, new volcanoes on Io!"
Galileo found more than 150 volcanoes on Io,
which is about the size of the Moon. And those
volcanoes put out an amazing amount of heat.
"One of Io's volcanoes, Loki, is more powerful
than all of Earth's volcanoes combined," said
Lopes. The volcanoes on Io are named after
gods and goddesses of fire and thunder. Lopes
got to name two of Io's volcanoes. She named
them Tupan and Monan, after gods in native
Brazilian mythology.

MAPPING VENUS AND THE MOON

Sometimes amazing discoveries are right in
your own backyard. NASA hadn't sent a spacecraft to the Moon in more than twenty years
when it launched *Clementine* in 1994. *Lunar
Prospector* soon followed in 1998. These small
probes mapped the surfaces of the Moon in all
sorts of ways. The orbiters made topographical
maps that showed the height of hills and
depths of craters. Maps of the kinds of minerals
and chemicals in lunar soil and of the Moon's
gravity were also created. It was worth the

work, because the maps revealed something
astonishing—water on the Moon. Water ice,
to be exact—five billions tons of it trapped in
the chilly shadows of the poles. Suddenly, the
idea of a human lunar colony seemed a lot less
like science fiction!

Magellan was another history-making mapping mission. It was the first probe launched
from a space shuttle in 1989, and it also broke
NASA's 10-year dry spell of sending no probes to
the planets. *Magellan* proved that there was still

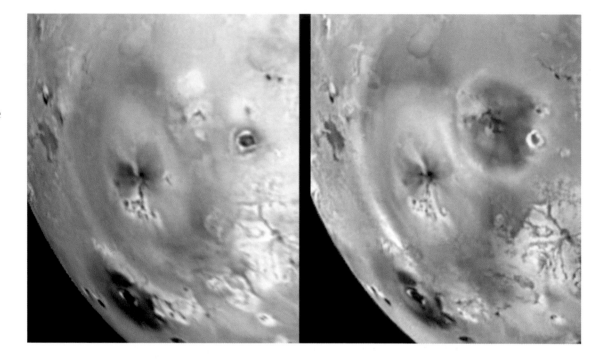

Left: *Galileo* took this picture of Io during its
seventh orbit around Jupiter. Right: This photo,
taken during *Galileo*'s tenth orbit around Jupiter,
shows a new, giant dark spot the size of Arizona.
It's a new massive eruption of Io's volcano
Pillan Patera.

a lot to learn, even from neighboring Venus.
Venus is so shrouded in clouds that its surface
has always been difficult to see. Even spacecraft
cameras can't cut though the haze. What *can*
see through the soup is radar, and that's what
Magellan used to make its maps. *Magellan* was
able to make three complete mapping cycles
while orbiting Venus from 1990 to 1994.

Unbelievably, *Magellan* sent back more data
about Venus during those years than all other
NASA planetary missions until that time combined! *Magellan*'s map of Venus is so detailed
that we know more about Venus's surface than
we do about parts of Earth's ocean floor!
Magellan's view of Venus shows a relatively
young world whose entire surface was repaved
with lava from planet-wide ancient volcanoes
about 500 million years ago. Those once-active
volcanoes left most of Venus covered in lava
plains, lava domes, and long lava channels.
The rest of Venus's surface is covered with odd-
looking, deformed mountains. *Magellan*'s maps
show no signs of water (past or present) and no
moving crustal plates or active volcanoes today.

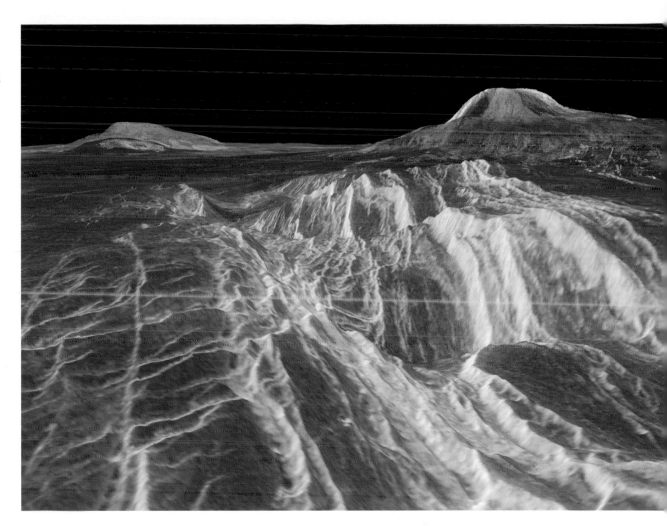

Magellan's mapping mission to Venus produced detailed 3-D images of the planet's ancient volcanoes, lava plains, and deformed mountains.

Metric Matters

activity

NASA lost a $125 million spacecraft because of a metric mix-up. The *Mars Climate Orbiter* burned up in Mars's atmosphere because it was mistakenly given a navigation command in pounds of rocket force, an English measurement unit. Because NASA's policy is to use only metric measurements, Mission Control assumed the command was in the standard metric unit of rocket force, or newtons. (One English pound of force equals 4.45 newtons.) The difference between pounds and newtons changed the orbiter's path of entry into Mars's atmosphere. The *Mars Climate Orbiter* came in too low, smashed into the planet's atmosphere, and burned up.

Measurements are meaningless unless units follow them. If you say, "I weigh 100," it doesn't mean much. One hundred what—kilograms, pounds, stones, ounces, tons, grams? Find out for yourself the difference that units can make in this activity.

YOU'LL NEED

Road atlas or map that has a scale in both miles and kilometers

Sticky note or other small scrap of paper

Pencil

1. Find your town or city on the map or atlas. Look for the legend box that has a scale in miles and kilometers.
2. Use the sticky note to create a distance ruler. Line up the top left corner of the sticky note to the 0 kilometers mark on the map's kilometers scale. Then mark and label the top edge of the sticky note at 100 kilometers. Next do the same for 100 miles on the note's bottom edge.
3. Let's say you plan to meet a friend 100 units east of your town. Use your distance ruler to measure 100 kilometers east of your town, and mark the spot with a pencil. Then use the distance ruler to mark the spot 100 *miles* east of your town. How far apart are they? Could you have met up without knowing the units of the distance?
4. Now let's say your plans have changed, and you're going to meet your friend 300 units east of town. Use the distance ruler to measure 300 kilometers east, and mark the spot with a pencil. Then use the distance ruler to mark the spot 300 miles east. How far apart are the two spots? What happens to the difference between distances when the numbers are multiplied?

MARS LOST

Mars may be our neighbor, but it's not an easy place to visit. On average, only one out of every three spacecraft sent to Mars is successful. (See page 149 for a time line of Mars missions.) In the 1990s that average was even worse. Of the eight missions to Mars launched during the decade, only two made it to the Red Planet—that's a 75 percent failure rate.

What happened? NASA's *Mars Observer*, the first spacecraft sent to that planet in 17 years, was only two days away from Mars when all contact with it was lost. Russia's *Mars '96* was supposed to land on Mars, but it ended up in the Pacific Ocean after a failed launch. And Japan's *Nozomi* ran out of fuel before engineers could get it into orbit around Mars. One of the more embarrassing Martian mishaps was the mistake made with NASA's *Mars Climate Orbiter* (see "Metric Matters" activity, at left). Unfortunately, the failures didn't end there! NASA's *Mars Polar Lander* and its companion microprobes, *Deep Space 2,* were also lost after it reached the Red Planet in late 1999. But all the failures were forgiven and forgotten for a time when a "little rover that could" named *Sojourner* cruised onto a dusty Martian surface. For humans, it was the best thing to happen on Mars since the Viking mission 20 years earlier.

The lander that carried the *Sojourner* rover to Mars was called *Mars Pathfinder*. Both arrived on a chilly July 4, 1997. It'd been a rough-and-tumble landing. As *Mars Pathfinder* parachuted down to the Martian surface from space, huge protective air bags inflated all over the lander. When *Mars Pathfinder* slammed into the ground at 30 miles (48 km) per hour, it bounced and rolled like a giant beach ball across the rusty ground. After finally coming to a stop, *Mars Pathfinder* deflated its air bags and opened its petal-like doors. Inside the open lander was a little six-wheeled rover the size of a microwave oven. *Sojourner* would become the first mobile vehicle ever to roam another planet.

MARS FOUND

All around the *Mars Pathfinder* lander were the endless reddish-brown rocks and dirt of Mars's Ares Vallis region. A pinkish sky hung overhead. *Mars Pathfinder* radioed news of its arrival back

to Earth and started snapping pictures. Then *Sojourner*'s motors began to whirr. The 23-pound (10-kg) toaster oven–sized rover was ready to roll! *Sojourner* slowly moved down a yellow ramp and rolled onto Mars, its spiky wheels leaving tread marks in the sandy dust. When the first pictures of *Sojourner* on Mars reached Earth, NASA engineers and scientists cheered and yelled with joy—and relief. Brian Cooper, *Sojourner*'s lead rover driver, was one of them. Cooper got ready to go to work. It was his job to control *Sojourner* on Mars.

Technicians close up *Mars Pathfinder*'s petal-like doors around the rover *Sojourner* a few weeks before its launch in 1996. It took only three years and $150 million to build and launch the mission—less time and money than was required to build other Mars spacecraft.

Sojourner checks out a rock named Yogi, after rolling down *Mars Pathfinder*'s yellow ramp in 1997.

Cooper said. "I used it to explore my living room." After college, Cooper went to work for NASA's Jet Propulsion Laboratory testing robot rovers, including *Sojourner*. With *Sojourner* safely on Mars, it was time to see if the rover—and its driver—were up to their jobs.

Cooper "drove" the rover using a computer. Wearing 3-D goggles, he sat in front of a screen that showed a virtual *Sojourner* and the landscape around it. These were created from pictures sent back by the *Mars Pathfinder* lander. "With my three-dimensional goggles on, it's as if I'm standing on Mars," Cooper explained. He used a ball-shaped joystick to move the virtual *Sojourner* back and forth between the rocks on the screen. "I can look at the panorama and move back and forth as if I'm right on the lander or down on the ground, at *Sojourner*'s perspective."

Once Cooper mapped out a safe route on the computer, he sent the directions to *Sojourner* on Mars. Controlling a rover that's millions of miles away isn't easy. It took at least 10 minutes for pictures and messages from Mars to reach Cooper on Earth. If engineers on Earth were

Controlling, or driving, a robot rover on Mars was a dream job for Cooper. As a kid he'd loved video games, magic tricks, and remote-controlled cars—as well as science fiction stories about robots and talking computers. When Cooper was nine years old he watched Neil Armstrong walk on the Moon, and he knew that he wanted to explore space, too. Cooper joined the air force, but poor eyesight kept him from becoming a pilot. He instead turned his interest in machines toward the study of engineering. "I built my first robot in college," watching pictures of *Sojourner* heading for a cliff, the lander would have already fallen off of it by the time they could get a STOP message to *Sojourner*. That's why Cooper used the computer to plan safe routes for *Sojourner* ahead of time, not in real time, as people do when they operate a remote-controlled car. "It's the safest way to drive on Mars," Cooper said.

Where did Cooper "drive" *Sojourner* to? For the most part, over to interesting rocks. Once it got up next to a rock, *Sojourner* would use its onboard cameras and science instruments to photograph and analyze it. *Sojourner* found out some amazing things about the rocks it examined. One came from a volcano, and others were once part of an ancient riverbed. It seems that Mars was, at one time, much more like Earth than it is today. But the "most fun was driving into areas that you couldn't see from the lander," Cooper said. "We could drive behind hills and see areas that were brand-new exploration. That could only happen with the rover."

The *Mars Pathfinder* mission was a huge success. The lander was designed to work for only a month, and *Sojourner* for a week.

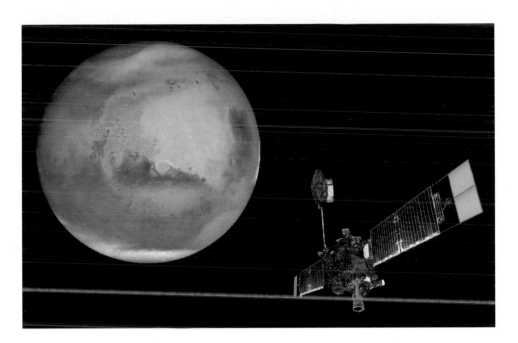

But apparently someone forgot to tell the rover that! *Sojourner* kept on roving for 12 weeks. And *Mars Pathfinder* kept sending back pictures—more than 16,500 in total—for three months until its batteries finally died. The *Mars Pathfinder* mission might have ended in 1997, but Brian Cooper kept working with rovers. Six years later he'd be back in the driver's seat, controlling NASA's next generation of rovers on Mars—*Spirit* and *Opportunity*.

Another successful Mars mission involved the *Mars Global Surveyor*. The orbiter arrived at Mars after *Mars Pathfinder* in 1997 and has been continually mapping and photographing the Red Planet ever since. Its images have given scientists more evidence that ancient Mars was wet.

2000s: Near-Earth Objects, Saturn's Rings, and Martian Seas

7

The *Cassini* space probe began its orbit of Saturn in 2004.

As the new millennium began on Earth, a dozen spacecraft were out exploring the solar system. *Galileo* orbited Jupiter, and *Cassini* grabbed a gravity boost on its way to Saturn. *Ulysses* circled the Sun's poles while the *Hubble Space Telescope* scanned the heavens from Earth's orbit. The *Mars Global Surveyor* mapped away as scientists built the next rovers bound for the Red Planet. In addition to the spacecraft of these major missions, there was also a flock of smaller, faster, cheaper spacecraft built by many different groups from a variety of countries out exploring the solar system. Many were part of NASA's new Discovery program.

The Discovery program works sort of like a contest. Anybody—labs, companies, universities, or space agencies— can send in their plan for a space mission that explores the solar system. The only rules are that the whole thing must cost less than $425 million and launch within three years. The winners get their missions paid for by NASA. A number of the earliest Discovery program winners were missions to some of the solar system's smallest worlds—asteroids.

BIG EVENTS ON SMALL WORLDS

Asteroids are small, rocky, airless worlds. Most asteroids orbit the Sun in a belt between Mars and Jupiter. While millions of asteroids make up the asteroid belt, some asteroids are closer to Earth. Asteroids (and comets) that orbit within Earth's neighborhood are called near-Earth objects (NEOs). And the very first Discovery mission was to pay a visit to an NEO— asteroid Eros.

The mission to Eros was called Near Earth Asteroid Rendezvous, or *NEAR*. The car-sized *NEAR* spacecraft began the first-ever orbit of an asteroid on Valentine's Day, 2000. (Eros is the Greek god of love, after all!) *NEAR* circled Eros, sending back 160,000 images of the asteroid's rocky surface. The solar-powered space probe measured Eros's size, mass, and odd, potato-like shape. It took gravity and magnetic field readings, and it also studied the asteroid's density.

After a year in orbit of Eros, *NEAR*'s main mission was complete. But the spacecraft was in good condition, so the *NEAR* team went for a big encore. They decided to try to make

111

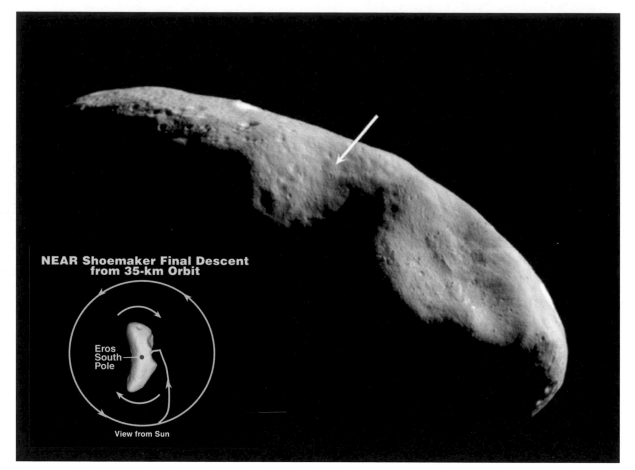

NEAR Shoemaker Final Descent from 35-km Orbit

Eros South Pole

View from Sun

NEAR Shoemaker orbited the asteroid Eros for a year, then landed on it (inset). The landing site is marked with an arrow in the photo of Eros (above).

NEAR the first ever spacecraft to land on an asteroid! *NEAR* was an orbiter, not a lander probe. But its team thought the probe could land on the asteroid without crashing. There's very little gravity on asteroids, and *NEAR*'s orbit wasn't all that high up. It was *NEAR* navigation team leader Bobby Williams's job to make it happen.

Williams recalled the day of the planned landing. "[W]e got a really early start at 2:00 A.M.," he said. "Everybody was pretty excited. It was like going in for your final exam, and you know you'll get an A." The team was going to have to calculate *NEAR*'s path down to the asteroid as it descended, sending the spacecraft corrections along the way. *NEAR* fired its thrusters four times on the way down to slow itself to a speed of 5 feet (1.6 m) per second. As *NEAR* neared the surface, it snapped 60 pictures, which showed golf ball– to truck-sized boulders on the asteroid's surface. Then the spacecraft set down. Not a single instrument on board was damaged. "The secret of success here is that we did our homework several times," Williams told reporters after the cheers in the control room had died down. *NEAR* continued to

Stardust collected comet dust by capturing it in a special material called aerogel, shown here.

send back information about Eros for another two weeks until it surrendered to the cold and dark.

NEAR wasn't the last probe to study an asteroid. A Japanese spacecraft called *Hayabusa* visited asteroid Itokawa in 2005. While there, it collected pieces of the asteroid and will return them to Earth during the summer of 2010. It'll be the first sample-return mission to an asteroid. And *Dawn*,

another spacecraft in the asteroid-bound Discovery mission, launched in late 2007. It will orbit the newly classified dwarf planet Ceres and asteroid Vesta, in the asteroid belt.

Discovery missions are also targeting the other kind of near-earth objects during this decade—comets. *Stardust* met up with a comet named Wild 2 in early 2004 and captured bits of its atmosphere's, or coma's, dust and gas. Then it returned the first collected comet samples to Earth. Another Discovery space probe recently went on a less gentle comet mission. When *Deep Impact* met up with the comet Tempel 1 in 2005, the probe launched a giant projectile into the comet. It blew out a crater as big as a football field and as deep as a seven-story building! Scientists are studying the findings that cameras and instruments on *Deep Impact* recorded after the blast. It has given them a unique look at what's inside the comet!

Near-earth objects (NEOs) have slammed into Earth in the past. An NEO likely killed off the dinosaurs 65 million years ago. That's one reason why scientists want to keep an eye on where NEOs are and find out more about them.

NASA's *Deep Space 1* (*DS1*) probe flew by the comet Borrelly in 2001, after first visiting the near-Earth asteroid Braille. *DS1* was successfully powered by an experimental ion propulsion system fueled by xenon gas.

The NEO Hunters

Remember Shoemaker-Levy 9, the comet that crashed into Jupiter (see page 99)? It was discovered by three famous comet hunters: Eugene and Carolyn Shoemaker and David Levy. Eugene Shoemaker (1928–1997) was a famous geologist and comet hunter. A month after *NEAR* started orbiting Eros, NASA renamed the spacecraft *NEAR Shoemaker* in his honor. His comet-hunting wife, Carolyn Shoemaker (b. 1929), has discovered 32 comets—more than anyone else alive today.

David Levy (b. 1948) is a writer and amateur comet hunter who's discovered 21 comets! Amateur comet hunters do what professional astronomers don't have time to do. They painstakingly scan the night sky with telescopes, searching for a faint smudge of light that has never been seen before. The heyday of amateur comet (and asteroid) hunters has passed, however. Most new NEOs are today found by computer-controlled automated search systems—robot telescopes! But human hunters do still make a couple of comet discoveries per year.

But comets and asteroids can also give us clues about the early solar system. They're 4.6-billion-year-old leftovers from the beginning of the solar system's formation. Unlike planets, comets and asteroids haven't changed much during all that time. They're like windows into the past.

STUDYING SATURN

Not every new space mission belongs to the smaller, faster, cheaper club. The first spacecraft to orbit Saturn is the most complicated machine ever sent to another world. The spacecraft, named *Cassini,* arrived at the ringed planet in 2004 and began its mission to study Saturn, its rings, and eight of its planet-like icy moons. "Saturn is almost like a miniature solar system," explained Linda Spilker. Studying a mini-solar system takes a big mission. Spilker is the *Cassini* mission's Deputy Project Scientist. She's been studying the solar system ever since she got her first telescope—at age nine!

Even though Spilker got good grades in her math and science classes, some people tried to talk her out of being a scientist. Not many women studied physics in the 1960s. But, said

Space scientist Linda Spilker started working on the *Cassini* mission nearly a decade before the spacecraft launched.

Spilker years later, "Alan Shepherd, John Glenn, and the walk on the Moon got me dreaming about being part of the space program." Her dream of exploring the planets with NASA came true when she got a job on the Voyager missions in 1977. Spilker has been working on the Cassini mission since 1988, nine years before *Cassini* even launched! "My responsibilities include helping the project put together the best science possible for the four years *Cassini* will spend in orbit around the planet Saturn,"

Catch and Count Falling Stars

activity

Those streaks of light In the night sky called falling or shooting stars are actually meteors. Meteors are chunks of space rock (meteoroids) that have fallen into a planet's atmosphere. Most meteoroids are chunks of long-gone comets or bits of broken-up asteroids. Cloud-like clusters of tiny meteoroids orbit the Sun. When the Earth passes through them they burn up in our atmosphere, creating meteor showers.

Earth travels through a number of these meteoroid clusters during the same time every year. Look at the chart below to see when the next meteor shower is. Then plan on catching the show. The best place to watch a meteor shower is the darkest place. Try to get away from city and highway lights, and choose a night when the Moon isn't full. Meteor showers are often named after the star constellations they appear in. Look for them in that constellation's part of the night sky. Astronomy and telescope magazines list star charts by month to point you in the right direction, and so do many sky calendar Web sites (see page 165). The Science at NASA Web site (http://science.nasa.gov) often lets meteor watchers know when an especially good shower is on the way, and it gives detailed sky maps to help you spot them.

YOU'LL NEED

Sleeping bag, blanket, or exercise mat

Bowl or cup

50 pennies

Timer or watch with alarm

1. Once you've figured out when and where to watch for falling stars, head outside. Take a sleeping bag, blanket, or exercise mat to lie on, and dress appropriately. Lie down in a position that lets you see the correct part of the night sky when you look up. Start looking for streaks of light!

2. Set the bowl or cup near your hand so you don't have to see it to find it.

3. Set the timer or watch alarm for 30 minutes. Hold some pennies in your hand and drop one in the cup each time you see a meteor during the next half hour.

4. At the end of the half hour, count the number of pennies in your cup and double that number to calculate your "meteors per hour" number. Compare the number to the chart at left. Did you see fewer or more meteors?

ANNUAL METEOR SHOWERS

Meteor Shower Name	Dates Seen (Peak Day)	Constellation Found In	Meteors per Hour
Quadrantids	Jan. 1–4 (Jan. 3)	Bootes	50
Lyrids	Apr. 19–23 (Apr. 21)	Lyra	10–15
Eta Aquarids	May 1–8 (May 4)	Aquarius	20
Delta Aquarids	July 26–31 (July 29)	Aquarius	25
Perseids	Aug. 10–14 (Aug. 12)	Perseus	60
Orionids	Oct. 18–23 (Oct. 22)	Orion	25
Taurids	Oct. 15–Dec. 1 (Nov. 1)	Taurus	15
Leonids	Nov. 14–20 (Nov. 17)	Leo	Varies
Geminids	Dec. 10–15 (Dec. 13)	Gemini	50

Giovanni Cassini (1625–1712)

The *Cassini* spacecraft is named after an Italian-born French 17th-century astronomer. Giovanni Cassini used early telescopes to study the planets. He measured how long a day was on Venus, Mars, and Jupiter by timing how long each planet took to spin one time. He discovered ice caps on Mars and Jupiter's Great Red Spot. Cassini also mapped the Moon and used triangulation to estimate the distances between both Earth and the Sun and Earth and Mars.

But Cassini is most famous for his Saturn discoveries. Using telescopes, he discovered four of Saturn's moons—Iapetus, Rhea, Tethys, and Dione. In 1675 Cassini discovered a large gap in Saturn's rings, which became known as the Cassini Division. He (correctly) thought that Saturn's rings weren't one big solid disk, as most people believed at the time. In fact, there are gaps between Saturn's seven rings that are large enough for visiting spacecraft to safely fly through—including *Cassini*.

explained Spilker. She's an expert on planetary rings, so the job is a perfect fit.

Cassini will orbit Saturn through at least 2008, flying by its moons and studying Saturn's rings with the most sophisticated science instruments ever sent into space. In early 2005 the *Huygens* atmospheric probe separated from *Cassini* and descended to Saturn's largest moon, Titan, right on schedule. *Huygens* took weather and atmospheric measurements and snapped pictures as it fell through Titan's smoggy atmosphere. It even survived on the surface for a couple of hours after setting down on orange, spongy sands along the coastline of a sea of liquid natural gas. What a place!

"Titan has an atmosphere that contains hydrocarbons and other compounds that may represent the building blocks for life," explained Spilker. "By studying Titan, we may get a better understanding of how life evolved on the early Earth." It's hoped that scientists will solve some of Titan's mysteries over the next few years thanks to *Huygens*'s historic mission.

Such a big mission called for a big spacecraft. *Cassini-Huygens* weighs more than six tons

Cassini has taken amazing images of Saturn. The false colors of Saturn's rings show their varying temperatures. Red rings are the least cool at about -262°F (-163°C), green are about -298°F (-183°C), and blue rings are the coldest, at about -334°F (-203°C).

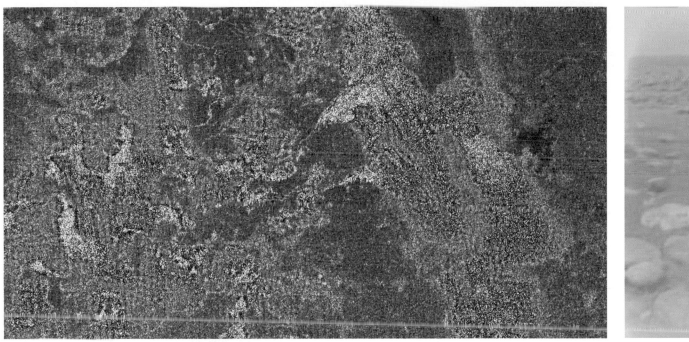

Far left: *Cassini*'s radar cut through Titan's haze to reveal a landscape of ridges and valleys. Left: *Huygens*'s first color picture from the surface of Titan.

(5,000 kg) and is about the size of a 30-person school bus! It's the largest spacecraft ever sent to the outer solar system, and it was built with international cooperation. While NASA built the *Cassini* orbiter, the Italian Space Agency chipped in its high-gain antenna. And the *Huygens* probe was built by the European Space Agency. In all, 17 nations helped build *Cassini-Huygens*. And hundreds of scientists around the world are studying the information and images that *Cassini* has sent back.

Cassini's discoveries quickly stacked up. The oversized orbiter discovered four new moons, and it found water-based ice and carbon dioxide–based "dry" ice on Saturn's moon Phoebe. This is strong evidence that Phoebe was once part of the faraway Kuiper belt, where many comets come from! *Cassini* also snapped pictures of Titan that show a haze that's "kind of an organic goo, much like the smog that one might see in Los Angeles," said Spilker. And Saturn's famous system of rings is proving to be even

more fascinating than ever before thought! No one is more excited about the ring discoveries than Linda Spilker. Understanding Saturn's rings and how they work is the focus of her research as a scientist.

"Saturn's rings are made up of millions of particles ranging in size from dust to large boulders," Spilker explained. "Many of these ring particles are affected by the moons that orbit outside them. The gravity from the moons causes the ring particles to bump into each other and

Put Together a Probe

activity

Space probes come in many different shapes and sizes. Flipping through this book, you'll find pictures of small rovers, giant orbiters, legged landers, and pod-like atmospheric probes. Each was created and designed to meet the needs of its own specific mission.

Choose one of the spacecraft you've learned about and build a model of it. You can do it in one of two ways. Use one of the patterns and instructions given on the Spacecraft Model Web sites on page 165. Or, build your own model using everyday materials. If you want to build your own, first study a picture of the spacecraft. What could you use for its parts? A juice box, paper towel tube, chunk of Styrofoam, or shoebox could be the probe's main body. Egg carton cups, paper bowls, or cupcake liners can be communication-dish antennas. You can protect the probe with a space-blanket covering of aluminum foil or gold wrapping paper. Rover wheels can be made of lids or balls of clay. Just use your imagination!

create interesting patterns in the rings, such as waves and wakes." *Cassini* found that, surprisingly, some of the rings are much warmer than others. And the spacecraft also discovered a never-before-seen ring. While learning about Saturn and its rings and icy moons is reason enough to send *Cassini* there, Spilker believes the spacecraft can do even more. "Studying planets like Saturn helps us understand more about the Earth," explained Spilker. "By studying the atmosphere and winds of a giant planet like Saturn, we may be able to better predict the Earth's weather." After all, we're all part of the same solar system.

WAS MARS ONCE WET?

For hundreds of years people have wondered, "Is there life on Mars?" But after more than three decades of sending spacecraft to the Red Planet, no plants, animals, or even microbes have been found. Is Mars simply too cold and dry for life? Water is essential to the chemistry of life as we know it. Anything that we're likely to recognize as life needs liquid water to exist. But that's the puzzle. While Mars is a frigid desert today, signs of ancient water are all over the place. It's like being in a dry desert streambed on Earth. There's not a drop of liquid water in sight. But all around are rocks tumbled smooth by water, water-carved channels in the sand, and crusty minerals left behind where puddles once stood. We know that water was once there.

The question of life on Mars is now focused on the past, when water did flow on the planet. Did an ancient, wetter, warmer Mars have life? Again, the answer probably depends on the water that was there. If all the now-dry river-beds and rain-eroded hillsides of Mars were created by once-a-millennium flash floods, the answer is probably no. Imagine an ice-filled comet delivering a load of water to Mars— along with quite a crater upon its impact! Rivers of water would flow and rain would fall until the liquid water disappeared into the planet's polar ice caps or evaporated out into space. (Remember, Mars doesn't have as much atmosphere-anchoring gravity and atmospheric pressure as Earth.) It would be hard for simple organic substances to evolve into life in this temporarily wet scenario. Even if Mars was

The *Mars Exploration Rover* (MER) (left) is larger, has more cameras, and carries more science instruments than does the smaller Sojourner-generation rover (right).

flooded repeatedly, how would life survive the long dry spells?

On the other hand, what if there were ancient oceans that existed for millions of years before they dried up? Now that would be a place where life might have had the time to evolve and thrive! Such a place exists on Mars. Meridiani Planum is a flat area near Mars's equator and east of its enormous Valles Marineris canyon.

Meridiani Planum is also the place where a rover named *Opportunity* rolled off its lander in 2004.

ROBOT ROCK HOUNDS

An unusual opportunity opened up to space explorers a while back. In 2003 Mars made its closest approach to Earth in 60,000 years. A spacecraft sent during this rare launch window would get to Mars in six short months.

Above left: *Opportunity* landed in Eagle Crater on Mars's Meridiani Planum in 2004 and left its lander behind to search for the mineral hematite. After the rover found the blueberry-shaped balls of gray hematite (above right), it used the rock abrasion tool (RAT) at the end of its arm to scour this circle in the rock surface and analyze what lay beneath.

(It had taken the Viking probes ten months, and *Mars Pathfinder* seven, to get to Mars.) NASA took advantage of the event by launching two twin spacecraft toward Mars in the summer of 2003. The Europeans launched *Mars Express* that summer as well. Both NASA spacecraft landed on Mars in January 2004, in the same less-than-elegant way that *Mars Pathfinder* had. They bounced and rolled, cushioned by giant airbags, until coming to a safe stop. It had been an inexpensive way to land *Mars Pathfinder*—why not use it again? But these newly landed Mars Exploration Rovers (MERs) weren't copies of *Mars Pathfinder*'s rover *Sojourner*. The two rovers—named *Opportunity* and *Spirit*—were something much better.

The golf cart–sized MERs had "more instruments, better cameras, and can go farther from the lander," explained Joy Crisp, who worked on the *Mars Pathfinder* mission during the 1990s. *Sojourner* traveled about the length of a football field during its entire mission. Each MER can go that distance every single day. Joy Crisp is now the Project Scientist for the MER mission. Crisp is a geologist, which makes her the perfect leader for the mission. *Opportunity* and *Spirit* are basically roving field geologists—they're robotic rock hounds! Crisp herself has been a rock hound since college. The fun field trips and interesting lab work convinced this devoted bookworm that geology was the career for her. "Studying rocks and pulling out clues as to how they were formed" is what's exciting about geology, explained Crisp. It's like solving a mystery. "I find this work fascinating on Earth, so figuring out these puzzles on Mars is even more exciting," she said.

Crisp's job as MER mission Project Scientist was to guide *Opportunity* and *Spirit* in their search for clues in the rocks of the Red Planet. "Some of the questions about Mars that we are trying to answer are: What were the environmental conditions like when the rocks formed? We are especially interested in the possibility if water existed or still does exist on Mars. . . . Was water only there for brief flooding episodes?" asked Crisp. This was why *Opportunity* landed at Meridiani Planum. Mars experts knew from past

Mars Exploration Rover (MER) scientist and geologist Joy Crisp.

Europe's Express Mission to Mars

Mars Express was the European Space Agency's first mission to another planet. It launched from Kazakhstan, arrived at Mars in late 2003, went into orbit, and released its *Beagle 2* lander toward the surface. Unfortunately, *Beagle 2* was never heard from again. Even though *Beagle 2* was lost, the *Mars Express* orbiter was fine. And *Mars Express* soon started making amazing discoveries. The orbiter took pictures that show evidence of a huge frozen sea just below Mars's surface near the equator. Could simple life forms, like microbes, live in this ice today? Mars's equator region is now a prime target for future landers. *Mars Express* also snapped images of what seem to be relatively recent active volcanoes! Onboard instruments have also detected methane (natural gas) in Mars's atmosphere. On Earth this gas often comes from microbes. Does finding methane mean there's life on Mars today? Maybe, or maybe not. But *Mars Express*'s amazing discoveries have definitely added to Mars's mysteries!

Opposite page: *Spirit* landed in Gusev Crater in 2004 and headed for the Columbia Hills, seen here on the right horizon. Once it reached the Columbia Hills seven months later, *Spirit* studied a rock named Clovis (left) by drilling holes in it and studying its minerals and chemical makeup. Tests showed that Clovis was probably once an underwater rock!

probes that a mineral called hematite was there. On Earth, gray hematite forms in wet places. Did *Opportunity* find water-formed gray hematite at Meridiani Planum? Yes it did, along with all kinds of other evidence that water had once been there. And not just occasionally flowing water—like eroded flash flood streambeds—but soaking, standing, percolating, seeping water.

The evidence? Not only are there odd, blueberry-shaped balls of gray hematite on the planet, but there are also mineral deposits like those left when water evaporates away. *Opportunity* landed in what scientists are pretty sure was once a salty Martian sea. Bingo!

Opportunity's twin rover, *Spirit*, wasn't quite as lucky early on. It set down on the

other side of Mars in Gusev Crater, a wide basin strewn with volcanic rocks. *Spirit* had a rough start. A couple of weeks after its landing, Mission Control lost contact with the rover. Engineers finally figured out that *Spirit* had a computer problem and was trying to fix itself by continually restarting. Because of this, the rover's battery was dangerously close to being ruined. That would kill *Spirit*. Everyone worked around the clock to save *Spirit* before it was too late. "Sleeping and eating were optional," recalled Mission Manager Mark Adler. "There were cots we could sleep on in our offices. This was our one objective, our primary objective in our lives, was to get our spacecraft back." Adler's team was finally able to put *Spirit* in a resting mode and find the malfunction in its flash memory. Engineers spent four days reprogramming parts of *Spirit*'s computer. Then they uploaded the same changes to *Opportunity*, which had just landed, before it suffered the same fate.

Healthier than ever, *Spirit* faced its next challenge—finding something interesting!

Spirit's bouncy landing left it far from the etched-looking bedrock that scientists hoped it'd check out. The twin MER rovers were supposed to last only three months. Would *Spirit* even make it over to the must-see bedrock by then? It didn't. But neither MER died on time, either. Six months into what turned out to be lifespans longer than three *years*, *Spirit* reached that bedrock in Gusev Crater, named the Columbia Hills—and hit pay dirt. *Spirit*'s extendable arm, which was full of science instruments, found that the rocks there had been changed by

Mars Reconnaissance Orbiter began orbiting the icy Martian poles in 2006.

water—lots of water. These were the kinds of changes that happen to rocks that are underwater for a long time. Gusev Crater was probably once a seabed or lakebed. Thanks to *Spirit* and *Opportunity*, there's no longer any doubt. Mars was once a much wetter and warmer world. And it's likely that parts of Mars were wet for long, possibly life-creating, periods of time.

MORE MARS, PLEASE

When Joy Crisp was asked why we should spend money on Mars missions, she answered, "So that we can all participate in a great adventure exploring this frontier. . . . A better understanding of Mars will help us find out new things about how the Earth evolved and how the Earth is changing today. What we learn by designing and carrying out missions to Mars will provide new ideas and newly inspired kids who become scientists and engineers to help solve problems we face on planet Earth." Crisp isn't the only one who thinks that exploring Mars is worth the price tag. More Mars missions are in the works for this decade. One is set to launch about every other year.

Next up was *Mars Reconnaissance Orbiter* (*MRO*). *MRO* began orbiting Mars in 2006. It's now scanning the Red Planet for signs of past or present water. On board are special sounder radar that are even searching for water under ground. The orbiter is equipped with the most powerful camera ever sent into space. It can send back images of surface features on Mars that are as small as a dinner plate! In addition to its role as a divining rod, *MRO* is studying the weather. *MRO* is also helping scientists find good landing sites for future missions—like that of *Phoenix*.

Phoenix is the next lander mission to Mars. It launched in 2007 and is set to arrive in 2008. *Phoenix* is the first of NASA's Scout program. It's a "smaller, faster, cheaper" contest program like Discovery, but this one focuses on exploring Mars. *Phoenix* will land in the one place where everyone is sure that water exists today on Mars—the icy northern pole. Could there be Martian microbes able to exist in such a cold place? *Phoenix* will look for clues by digging trenches in the ice with a robotic arm and searching for signs of life on Mars.

Phoenix won't have a bouncy airbag-assisted landing on Mars like that of *Mars Pathfinder* and *MER*. It will softly set down in a specific place, thanks to a dozen descent engines.

See Mars in 3-D

activity

The cameras on *Mars Pathfinder*'s rover, *Sojourner*, as well as those aboard *Sprit* and *Opportunity*, took three-dimensional (3-D) pictures. These help scientists see depth and distance—and they are really cool to look at! The landscapes and rocks seem to jump right off the page. You need 3-D glasses to view these kinds of pictures. Make your own pair in this activity. You'll get a brand new view of the Red Planet.

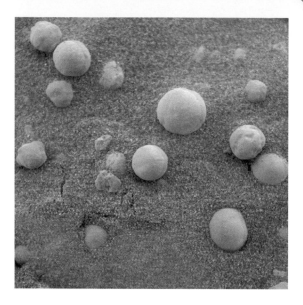

YOU'LL NEED

7" x 5" (18-cm x 13-cm) piece of light-weight cardboard (such as from a cereal box) or poster board

Scissors

Tape or glue

2" x 1¼" (5-cm x 3.5-cm) piece of red cellophane*

2" x 1¼" (5-cm x 3.5-cm) piece of blue cellophane*

* You can buy cellophane at craft or art supply stores. If cellophane is not available, you can use red and blue plastic report covers instead, as long as they're transparent and objects don't appear blurry when you look through them.

1. Set a photocopy machine to enlarge by 200 percent, and copy the three pattern pieces at right.

2. Use the patterns to cut pieces out of the cardboard (one piece for each pattern). Don't forget to cut out the eye ovals!

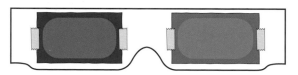

3. Tape or glue the red piece of cellophane onto the back of the left eye opening.

4. Tape or glue the blue piece of cellophane onto the back of the right eye opening.

5. Fold the end tabs on the eyepiece, using the dashed lines on the pattern as guides.

6. Tape or glue the earpieces to the eyepiece. Your 3-D glasses are ready!

7. Try out your glasses on the picture of the Martian soil above right. You can find more of *Spirit*'s and *Opportunity*'s 3-D images of Mars at http://marsrovers.nasa.gov/gallery/3d. You can browse 3-D images from around the solar system at http://photojournal.jpl.nasa.gov/feature/3-d and at http://nix.nasa.gov (search for "3-D").

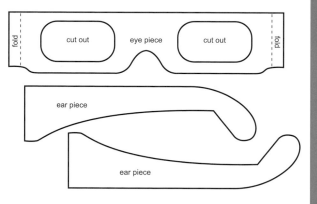

New Worlds and New Definitions

In 2005 Mike Brown and his team of astronomers announced that their giant telescope had spotted a tenth planet! The ice covered world, later named Eris, is bigger than Pluto and has its own small moon, named Dysnomia. The newly found world is about three times as far from the Sun as Pluto. In Greek mythology, Eris is the goddess of discord and strife, famous for starting fights. And that's exactly what calling Eris the tenth planet did. Many astronomers cried foul. They said there was no way that Eris was a true planet. Eris is a Kuiper belt object (KBO), after all. It's just one of billions of chunks of ice and rock out past Neptune in the Kuiper belt. But the problem was that if big KBOs like Eris aren't planets, neither is Pluto. Pluto is much more like a king-sized KBO than it's like any of the other eight planets. Astronomers have always considered Pluto an oddball. It doesn't fit in with either the four rocky terrestrial inner planets or the four gas giant outer planets. No one knew about KBOs when Pluto was discovered in 1930. But in 2002 astronomers discovered a big icy world in the Kuiper belt, named Quaoar. In 2003 an even bigger KBO, named Sedna, was found even farther away. So are all big KBOs like Eris and Pluto planets—or none? And if big KBOs are planets, are other big space objects like the asteroid Ceres planets, too?

The International Astronomical Union (IAU) settled the debate in 2006. After much strife and discord, IAU members decided that a space object needs three things to be a true planet. It must orbit the Sun, be big enough for gravity to squash it into a round ball, and have cleared other things out of its orbital neighborhood. Only Mercury, Venus, Earth, Mars, Jupiter, Saturn, Uranus, and Neptune fit the new definition—our solar system's eight planets. Pluto and Eris might be round and orbit the Sun, but their neighborhood is full of other KBOs. Likewise, Ceres orbits within the crowded asteroid belt. The IAU recognizes that big round space objects like Pluto and Eris are more than just simple space rocks. So they created a new category called dwarf planets for round space objects that orbit the Sun within a crowded neighborhood. There are three official dwarf planets—Eris, Pluto, and Ceres—with a dozen or so additional worlds under consideration, including Quaoar and Sedna. But don't get overly

An illustration of dwarf planet Eris and the faraway, faint Sun.

attached to the new definition of planet and dwarf planet. One or both could again change in the future. Scientists will keep finding new objects both at the edges of our solar system and circling around other suns. New discoveries will likely one day bring up an old question, "What exactly is a planet?"

8 ▶ 2010s: Going to Extremes

We've learned a lot about our solar system since the days when Galileo Galilei first gazed through his telescope at the phases of Venus's and Jupiter's moons. Earthlings have sent some 50 space missions to visit and study the planets of our solar system. The first space probes just flew by, grabbing what information they could and snapping quick pictures. Orbiters later followed, mapping landscapes in detail and tracking weather over time. And landers and atmospheric probes have given us an even closer look at many of the planets. Their discoveries have astounded the people who sent the space probes. "As we flew missions across the solar system, we constantly saw our socks knocked off," said planetary scientist Alan Stern. The robotic explorers' findings changed what everyone knew about the other worlds out there.

But there's one world that's never been on any probe's itinerary in all the decades since spaceflight started—Pluto. Everything we know about Pluto we know because of ground-based observations with telescopes, as well as space telescopes like the *Hubble*. But Pluto is hard to observe, even from Earth's orbit. It's really far away, for one thing—39 times farther than the distance between the Sun and Earth. Telescopes also have trouble peering at Pluto because its frost-covered surface reflects so much light. It's like trying to see something in a snowfield on a blindingly sunny day. And yet, some parts of Pluto are darker than coal. Other puzzling clues about Pluto have astronomers suspecting that there are ice- and gas-spewing geysers and a comet-like atmosphere around this newly reclassified dwarf planet. But the answers to most of Pluto's puzzles won't be solved until a spacecraft can get a closer look. Luckily, one is on its way.

LONG OVERDUE VISIT

New Horizons launched in 2006. It will become the first spacecraft to visit Pluto when it finally arrives around 2015. "Pluto is put up or shut up time in a way," explained Alan Stern. "It's a chance for us to now see if we can get [Pluto] right, and that's an irresistible challenge for a scientist." It's a challenge that Stern has taken on. He's the mission's Principal Investigator, the person in charge. Stern, like many of today's space scientists, got excited about space exploration as a kid

New Horizons will be the first spacecraft to visit Pluto and its moon Charon.

129

watching the Moon landings. "John Young, Dave Scott, and Harrison Schmitt, Apollo astronauts, all inspired me. . . and Carl Sagan," said Stern. Stern didn't just become a planetary scientist. He's also a pilot, and he was even a shuttle astronaut candidate for a while. But getting *New Horizons* ready to go to Pluto takes up most of his time these days.

"The first mission to explore Pluto is really important," said Stern. Not only will *New Horizons* explore Pluto, but it will also study some of the other icy mini-worlds of the Kuiper belt. Although astronomer Gerard Kuiper suggested in the 1950s that just such a belt existed, no one actually discovered any other KBOs until the 1990s. Scientists believe that KBOs are 4.6-billion-year-old leftover "building blocks" from when the planets formed. The Kuiper belt "holds clues to the origin of our outer solar system," explained Stern. "It's sort of an archaeological dig into the early history of our solar system."

The space probe *New Horizons* will have to travel a long way to reach Pluto. Weighing about half a ton (465 kg), the compactly built, piano-sized spacecraft is heavier than the early Pioneer probes, but smaller than the Voyagers. It took a year for *New Horizons* to reach Jupiter. While at the solar system's largest world in 2007, it made a flyby and grabbed a gravity boost that flung it toward Pluto. The trip from Jupiter to Pluto will take at least eight years—maybe ten. During much of that long cruise, *New Horizons* will be in a kind of electronic hibernation. All its unneeded systems will shut down. Stern and his team on Earth will wake

Pluto and its largest moon, Charon, are similar in size and close to each other. These *Hubble Space Telescope* images of Pluto and Charon (above) and their surfaces (below) are the best views we have so far.

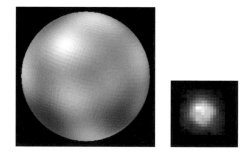

the spacecraft up once a year for a number of weeks to test its systems, make course corrections, and do anything else that needs to be done. But the main goal during the long cruise will be to just keep *New Horizons* healthy and ready for Pluto.

Once near Pluto, *New Horizons* will wake up and get to work. Even when it's 75 days away from its closest swing past Pluto, *New Horizons* will be able to capture images better than anything the *Hubble* has given us. Once it's near Pluto, the spacecraft will study both the dwarf planet and its moons. Instruments on *New Horizons* will map Pluto's and Charon's terrain in full color, map their surface temperatures, and analyze their atmospheres. Then the spacecraft will head for the nearest KBO. "With Pluto and the Kuiper belt, it's wide open," said Stern. "It's like the Wild West. You get to be the first to do things." One of those firsts will be the first exploration of a dwarf planet of the solar system.

An artist's view from the surface of one of Pluto's newly discovered small moons, Hydra and Nix. In the sky are Pluto (left), Charon (right), and the other small moon (far left). *New Horizons* will map all three of Pluto's moons.

My Mars Mission

activity

The goal of NASA's Mars Scout program is to get engineers and scientists to think up new designs for smaller, less expensive space probes that can be built quickly. The *Phoenix* lander will be the first Mars Scout design to land on Mars, but others are on the drawing board—and some of them are pretty weird! One calls for an airplane to drop out of the probe as the spacecraft enters Mars's atmosphere. As the plane drops off, its wings unfold and it starts flying over Mars. Another design has a balloon separating from a probe in midair. After filling itself with gas from a tank, the balloon drifts over Mars, taking pictures and measuring the weather. How about bringing some of Mars's air back to Earth? One Mars Scout idea calls for a bullet-like space probe to dip down into Mars's atmosphere, then quickly fly back to Earth, bringing its collected air and dust samples with it.

NASA is always looking for new ideas and designs for its Mars Scout program. What's yours? Think of a mission to Mars and a new kind of spacecraft that would be perfect for the job. Then write up the mission and draw its design on paper. Don't forget to give it a catchy name—and a low budget!

MESSENGER TO MERCURY

Mercury is an odd and largely ignored world. The only spacecraft to visit the first planet from the Sun was *Mariner 10*—in 1974! The images from *Mariner 10* showed a cratered, Moon-like, airless world that had cooked down to a mostly iron core. *Mariner 10* could photograph only half of Mercury during its three flybys, so there's a lot about the planet that we still don't know. It's a hard place to get to because of the strong gravity and powerful heat of the super-close Sun. And it's a hard planet to observe with a telescope. There's too much sun glare. Even the *Hubble* doesn't dare look Mercury's way. The intense solar radiation might fry its electronics.

The things we have learned about Mercury since *Mariner 10*'s voyage make the solar system's smallest planet seem even odder. It might be hard to imagine, but radar telescopes on Earth have spotted ice on Mercury. It seems that ice survives deep inside steep-walled craters near Mercury's poles. Scientists think that the ice is in the permanent shadow of the crater walls, so sunlight never reaches it.

Mercury's deep craters.

Like the airless Moon, Mercury bakes on its sunny side and freezes where no sunlight hits. But the presence of ice on a world where the Sun is eleven times brighter than it is on Earth is astonishing.

MESSENGER (above) will orbit Mercury for a year. Its protective sunshade is made of a high-tech, heat-resistant ceramic fabric. Will it find ice hiding in Mercury's deep craters (above left)?

Make a Mission Patch

activity

Mission patches are a great space-exploration tradition. Space agencies design a unique mission insignia, or patch, for every new mission. The insignia is used for many things—from decorating documents and posters to being sewn onto flight suits and engineer jackets. It's a symbol that represents the mission.

Take a look at a few of the past missions' patches here. They come in all shapes! The names of the astronauts are often part of the insignias for crewed missions. Sometimes the spacecraft or its destination is featured on the insignia. Mission patches aren't always serious, either. Cartoon characters including

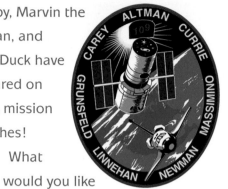

Snoopy, Marvin the Martian, and Daffy Duck have appeared on NASA mission patches!

What would you like to see on a future mission patch? Choose a future mission mentioned in this chapter, such as *New Horizons* or *Mars Science Laboratory*. Or invent and name a future mission you'd like to see happen, such as a crewed mission to Mars or a rover on Pluto. Then design an insignia to represent the mission. You can draw or paint the patch design, or create it on a computer using art software.

A spacecraft that will shed some light on these mysteries is now on its way to Mercury. *Mercury Surface, Space Environment, Geochemistry, and Ranging* (*MESSENGER*) will begin orbiting Mercury in 2011 after a long, roundabout, seven-year journey than includes some flybys. The small, solar-powered spacecraft will take pictures, map Mercury's surface, study its magnetic field, and find out what kinds of rocks and soil it has. *MESSENGER* is also equipped with a special sunshade to keep its electronics and instruments from overheating. It'll need it!

Not long after NASA's *MESSENGER* becomes the first spacecraft to orbit Mercury, the European and Japanese space agencies will launch two Mercury orbiters of their own. The joint mission is called BepiColombo, after Professor Giuseppe "Bepi" Colombo, the Italian mathematician who helped make *Mariner 10* a success. The European *Mercury Planetary Orbiter* will study the surface and chemical makeup of the planet. The Japanese *Mercury Magnetospheric Orbiter* will study Mercury's odd magnetic field. The least-explored inner planet is finally getting the attention it's due!

Engineers test the *MESSENGER* spacecraft before its 2004 launch.

MARS SHUTTLE

The goal to launch a spacecraft to Mars every other year continues at least through the next 20 years or so. The first to arrive in the 2010s decade will probably be *Mars Science Laboratory* (*MSL*). It's scheduled to land on the Red Planet in 2010 or 2011. *Mars Science Laboratory* will be a rover that can survive on Mars for at least an entire Martian year. That's 687 days on Earth.

Astronauts on Mars?

In late 2006 NASA announced it wants to send astronauts to Mars—from the Moon. NASA plans to start building a permanent lunar base in 2020. Many believe that lunar living will develop the technology needed for a crewed Mars mission. What would it take to get humans to Mars?

A trip to Mars is a 50-million-mile (80-million-km) journey. Any spacecraft that could be built with today's technology would take six to nine months to reach Mars—even if it started from a Moon base. Hopefully future propulsion systems will cut down on that time. The spacecraft would also have to carry a lot of food and water for such a long voyage. European Space Agency scientists estimated that six astronauts on a two-year round-trip Mars mission would need to take along 30 tons of food!

Being stuck in a small spacecraft for two years is no big deal for a robot rover. But it's a long time for humans to be cooped up. We've learned a lot about what happens to the human body during space flight from space station and shuttle mission astronauts. Floating around in microgravity looks like fun, but it's hard on the body. Astronauts get backaches and stomachaches from their bones and organs moving around inside them. Some nutrients are harder for the body to absorb in space. Astronauts' muscles weaken in space, too. Living and working with the same people in the same small, cramped space for a long time gets boring. It makes many people feel tired, irritable, depressed, or even hostile.

Many of these physical and mental problems aren't a big deal during a month-long mission. But some would likely become big problems on a longer trip. Exercise, certain medications, and special nutrients might be able to help astronauts go the distance and arrive at the Red Planet healthy. Some scientists are also looking into ways that humans might be put into a kind of "hibernation" sleep for part of the trip. But at the moment, that's just an idea. If you were among the first astronauts chosen to go to Mars, how would you want to travel there?

Its mission will be to specifically search for signs of life—fossil or living. Where will *MSL* land and look for life? That depends on what the Mars missions that take place between now and then find. Hopefully those spacecraft will spot a good site to send *MSL* to search.

More Mars Scout missions will also no doubt head to Mars during the 2010s. These small missions—which are chosen through a competitive contest—will probably be some of the oddest! There's everything on the drawing board from landers that dig down deep to look for Martian water to floating balloons and robotic airplanes!

We've learned a lot about Mars over the past 40 years, thanks to robotic space probes. But scientists won't be satisfied until they can see and study a chunk of Mars for themselves. A mission to bring Martian rocks and soil back to Earth will happen someday. Right now, the earliest return date for a Mars sample-return mission is probably 2014. No matter when it happens, it will be another big step in the exploration of our solar system.

Above: The Mars Sample-Return mission will bring a bit of Mars back to Earth. Left: The *Mars Science Laboratory* rover will look for life.

Field Guide to the Solar System

The following pages are your guide to the Sun, planets, Moon, dwarf planets, asteroids, and comets of our solar system. Here are some useful definitions and explanations to help you get the most out of the guide.

- **Diameter** is the measurement of a sphere. It's the distance through the center of the planet or moon at its equator.

- **Mass** is the measurement of the amount of an object's matter. In this guide, each planet's mass is described in comparison to Earth's own mass.

- **Gravity** is the pulling force between objects. The more mass an object has, the more gravity pulls on it. Earth has more gravity than the Moon because Earth has more mass. In this guide, gravity is described as it acts on the mass of a kid. That's what weight is.

- Planets spin, or rotate, like a top. The time it takes to make one spin, or **rotation**, is that planet's day length. Planets also travel around the Sun and moons around their planets. The time it takes a planet to make one trip, or orbit, around the Sun is that planet's year length.

- **Temperatures** listed in this guide are surface temperatures. Each terrestrial planet's coldest and hottest recorded temperatures are listed.

Effective temperatures are shown for the gas giants and for the Sun.

- The years listed in the Exploration Time Lines that note spacecraft events are generally the years of encounter, or when the spacecraft flew by, landed, or began its orbit. The spacecraft's encounter often occurred years after the launch date. More information about many of the spacecraft missions and important discoveries that are mentioned in the Exploration Time Lines can be found in chapters 1–8 (use the index to look up page numbers). The Web sites of ongoing and future spacecraft missions are listed in parentheses in the Exploration Time Lines.

Sun

Symbol:

Color: yellow

Diameter: 864,400 miles (1.4 million km)

Mass: equal to about 332,900 Earths

Gravity: an 85-pound (38.5kg) kid would weigh 2,380 pounds (1,078 kg)

Position: Milky Way galaxy

Rotation (Day Length): 609 hours

Composition: 92 percent hydrogen; 8 percent helium

Temperature: 9,939°F (5,504°C)

WHAT'S IT LIKE?

The Sun is a huge bright ball of ionized hydrogen and helium gas, or plasma. It's a medium-sized, middle-aged, yellow star. Its center, or core, is so hot that atoms fuse and release huge amounts of energy. Every second the Sun radiates an amount of energy that is equivalent to 100 billion tons of dynamite exploding! The average temperature of the Sun's "surface," or photosphere, is a mild 9,939°F (5,504°C). But it gets hotter in the Sun's outer layer, or corona. There temperatures average about 4,000,000°F (2,200,000°C).

SOLAR FACTS

- There are millions of other stars like the Sun in the Milky Way galaxy, and there are billions of other galaxies in the universe.

- Almost the entire mass of the solar system—99.86 percent—is that of the Sun. All the other objects in our solar system combined make up the other .14 percent!

- The Sun makes life on Earth possible by powering photosynthesis.

- The Sun's star name is Sol, after the Roman god of the sun.

- More than a million Earths could fit inside the Sun.

- The solar wind is a stream of charged particles that are constantly released by the Sun's corona.

- A solar eclipse happens when the Moon gets between the Sun and the Earth, blocking our view of the Sun.

- **Never** look right at the Sun—even with sunglasses on. It can hurt your eyes. Many believe Galileo Galilei lost his sight by looking directly at the Sun.

SUN EXPLORATION TIME LINE

PREHISTORY Humans observe its movements across the sky as it creates day and night

2137 B.C. Chinese astronomers record a solar eclipse

585 B.C. Thales of Miletus is first to predict a solar eclipse

A.D. 140 Ptolemy proposes that the Sun circles the Earth

1543 Copernicus states that the Sun is the center of the cosmos

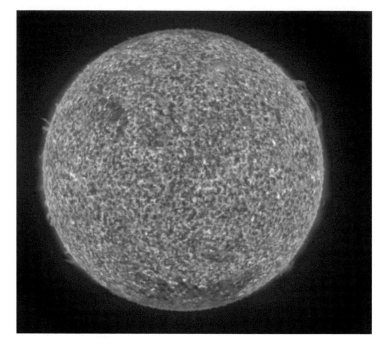

1610 Galileo Galilei observes sunspots with his telescope

1854 Scientists link solar activity to geomagnetic activity

1868 Astronomers detect helium in solar spectrum

1942 Astronomers observe radio emissions from Sun

1946 Astronomers measure the corona temperature to be 1,800,000°F (999,700°C).

1958 *Pioneer 1*, the first spacecraft launched by NASA, fails to reach the Moon, but discovers the solar wind

1973–1974 NASA's *Skylab* space station observes the Sun and discovers coronal holes

1975–1976 West German solar probes launched by NASA, *Helios 1* and *Helios 2*, come within 26 million miles (43 million km) of the Sun

1982 NASA's *Solar Maximum* probe makes solar flare observations

1991 Japanese satellite *Yohkoh* studies x-rays and gamma rays

1994–1995; 2000–2001 *Ulysses*, in a joint mission by the European Space Agency and NASA, studies polar regions of the Sun

1995 *Solar and Heliospheric Observatory* (*SOHO*), in a joint mission by the European Space Agency and NASA, studies the Sun's interior, atmosphere, and wind

1998 NASA's *Transition Region and Coronal Explorer* (*TRACE*) satellite observes the Sun's photosphere, transition region, and corona

2004 NASA's sample-return probe *Genesis* crashed upon its return to Earth after spending three years collecting solar wind particles, but its cargo was largely recovered

2007 NASA's *STEREO* (*Solar TErrestrial RElations Observatory*) spacecraft takes first-ever 3-D images of the Sun (http://stereo.jhuapl.edu)

2008 NASA's *Solar Dynamics Observatory* satellite to begin studying solar activity, space weather, and their impacts on Earth (http://sdo.gsfc.nasa.gov)

Mercury

Symbol:

Color: gray

Moons: none

Rings: none

Diameter: 3,032 miles (4,878 km)

Mass: about one-eighteenth (5.5 percent) of Earth's

Gravity: an 85-pound (38.5-kg) kid would weigh 32 pounds (15 kg)

Position: first planet from Sun

Distance from Sun: 36 million miles (57.9 million km)

Rotation (Day Length): 1,407 hours

Orbit (Year Length): 88 Earth days

Atmosphere: trace amounts of oxygen, sodium, and helium

Surface: rock

Minimum/Maximum Temperature: -279°F/801°F (-173°C/427°C)

WHAT'S IT LIKE?

Mercury is a lot like Earth's Moon. It's a small, nearly airless world of rocks, high cliffs, deep valleys, and craters (some of which are hundreds of miles wide). There's hardly any atmosphere, so the sky is always black. The Sun's rays are 10 times stronger on Mercury than on Earth, and the Sun looks three times as big. As on the Moon, the lack of air means that

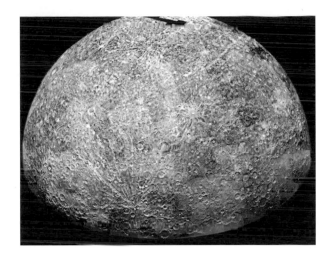

Mercury gets hot enough to melt lead during the day and cold enough for extreme freezer burn at night. Mercury's odd orbit and strange spin cause the morning Sun to rise briefly, then set and rise again. The reverse happens at sunset!

MERCURIAL FACTS

- Mercury is the smallest and fastest planet in the solar system, taking only 88 days for it to circle the Sun—its year. Mercury travels at 104,000 miles (167,400 km) per hour!

- Mercury may be the closest planet to the Sun, but it's not the hottest. Venus gets hotter, thanks to its carbon dioxide atmosphere.

- Atoms of oxygen, sodium, and helium are blasted off Mercury's surface by the solar wind. But they quickly escape into space, leaving the planet pretty much airless.

- Some of Mercury's deep craters are always shadowed and likely shelter ancient water-based ice that was left there by comets.

- To see Mercury, look for a planet that is close to the horizon in the western sky during the hour after sunset, or in the eastern sky during the hour before sunrise.

- Mercury's largest meteorite impact crater, Caloris Basin, is as wide as Texas.

- Mercury was named for the Roman messenger god who zipped around on winged sandals.

MERCURY EXPLORATION TIME LINE

PREHISTORY Humans observe its movements across the night sky

1610 Galileo Galilei observes Mercury through a telescope

1639 Giovanni Zupus discovers that Mercury has phases

1889 Giovanni Schiaparelli draws maps of Mercury's surface

circa 1900 Astronomers incorrectly declare that Mercury is in synchronous rotation (that it rotates once per orbit, every 88 days)

1965 Radar astronomers Gordon Pettengill and Rolf Dyce disprove the synchronous rotation theory and determine that Mercury's rotation is about 59 Earth days

1968 *Surveyor 7*—NASA lunar probe takes pictures of Mercury from the Moon

1974–1975 *Mariner 10*—NASA flyby probe is the first spacecraft to use a gravity assist and the first to fly by Mercury; it takes 10,000 images, capturing about 57 percent of the planet, during three separate passes and records surface temperatures from -297°F to 369°F (-183°C to 187°C)

1991 Radar astronomers on Earth detect water-based ice deep inside dark craters near Mercury's poles

2008–2009 *MESSENGER*—NASA's *Mercury Surface, Space Environment, Geochemistry and Ranging* orbiter, launched in 2004, makes a number of flybys before orbiting in 2011 (http://messenger.jhuapl.edu)

2019 Europe's and Japan's *BepiColombo* orbiters to map Mercury and investigate its magnetosphere after a 2013 launch (www.esa.int/science/bepicolombo)

Venus

Symbol:

Color: orange

Moons: none

Rings: none

Diameter: 7,521 miles (12,104 km)

Mass: about four-fifths (80 percent) of Earth's

Gravity: An 85-pound (38.5-kg) kid would weigh 77 pounds (35 kg)

Position: second planet from Sun

Distance from Sun: 67 million miles (107.8 million km)

Rotation (Day Length): 5,832 hours

Orbit (Year Length): 225 Earth days

Atmosphere: 97 percent carbon dioxide; 3 percent nitrogen

Surface: rock

Minimum/Maximum Temperature: 835°F/900°F (446°C/482°C)

WHAT'S IT LIKE?

With an average temperature of 867°F (464°C), it's hot enough to melt metal. The air's poisonous carbon dioxide acts as a blanket, trapping the heat. The orange sky is completely covered with yellow clouds made of sulfuric acid droplets that produce lightning and hurricane-force winds high up in the planet's atmosphere. Due to Venus's thick atmosphere, the air pressure at the planet's surface is 90 times that of Earth. Standing on Venus would feel like being 3,000 feet (900 m) under water, and winds would feel more like waves.

VENUSIAN FACTS

- Venus is sometimes called Earth's twin. It's the nearest planet to Earth, and it's about the same size.

- It's hotter than Mercury, thanks to runaway global warming caused by its carbon dioxide atmosphere. Its oceans boiled away long ago.

- Venus is home to thousands of ancient volcanoes. Much of the land was resurfaced 300–500 million years ago by lava flows.

- A day on Venus lasts 243 Earth days.

- Its rotation isn't only slow, it's backward. The Sun rises in the west and sets in the east on Venus.

- Its thick clouds reflect lots of sunlight into space, making Venus the second-brightest object in our night sky (the brightest object is the Moon).

- Landers on Venus only survive a few hours before being crushed by the pressure of the atmosphere.

- The planet, which is seen at sunset in the western sky, is called the evening star.

- Venus was named after the Roman goddess of love, and its symbol is the symbol for "female." Almost all of its canyons and craters are named after famous women, such as Sacagawea.

VENUS EXPLORATION TIME LINE

PREHISTORY Humans observe its movements across the night sky

1609 Using a telescope, Galileo Galilei studies the phases of Venus

1665 Giovanni Cassini determines the length of a day on Venus

1761 Mikhail V. Lomonosov uses a telescope to discover Venus's atmosphere when Venus passes in front of the Sun

1927 Using ultraviolet photographs, William H. Wright and Frank E. Ross discover Venus's clouds

1932 Walter S. Adams and Theodore Dunham, using infrared images, determine that Venus's atmosphere is mostly carbon dioxide

1950s Venus's high temperatures are discovered through the use of microwave radiation imaging

1961 Radar observations made using radio telescopes reveal Venus's slow spin

Soviet impact probe *Sputnik 7* fails to reach Venus

Soviet probe *Venera 1* is the first to fly to Venus, but contact is lost before its arrival

1962 NASA's *Mariner 1*, bound for Venus, fails during its launch

Soviet flyby probe *Sputnik 19* fails to reach Venus

NASA probe *Mariner 2* makes the first successful flyby of Venus, scans its surface from 21,620 miles (34,800 km), and confirms a temperature of 800°F (427°C)

Soviet flyby probes *Sputnik 20* and *Sputnik 21* fail to reach Venus

1964 Soviet flyby probes *Venera 1964A* and *Venera 1964B* fail during launch

Soviet flyby probe *Cosmos 27* fails to reach Venus

Soviet probe *Zond 1* travels to Venus, but contact is lost before its arrival

1965 Soviet probe *Venera 1965A* fails during launch

In this false-color map of Venus's surface, red areas indicate mountains; blue areas indicate deep valleys.

1966 Contact is lost with *Venera 2* before its arrival at Venus

Venera 3 is the first probe to impact the surface of another planet, but contact is lost

Soviet probe *Cosmos 96* fails during launch

1967 *Venera 4* is the first probe to explore the atmosphere of another planet; it confirms that Venus's atmosphere is carbon dioxide

Mariner 5 passes within 2,423 miles (3,900 km) of Venus's surface and detects its carbon dioxide atmosphere

Soviet probe *Cosmos 167* fails during launch

1969 Soviet atmospheric probes *Venera 5* and *Venera 6* report that Venus's atmosphere is 93 to 97 percent carbon dioxide

1970 Soviet lander *Venera 7* is the first spacecraft to send back data from the surface of another planet

Soviet probe *Cosmos 359* fails to reach Venus

1972 Soviet lander *Venera 8* measures the high winds of Venus's upper atmosphere as it descends to the planet's surface

Soviet probe *Cosmos 482* fails to reach Venus

1974 NASA flyby probe *Mariner 10* records circulation in Venus's atmosphere

1975 Soviet lander *Venera 9* is the first spacecraft to send photos from the surface of another planet, and its orbiter is the first spacecraft to orbit another planet

Soviet lander and orbiter *Venera 10* successfully orbited and set down on Venus

1978 NASA orbiter *Pioneer Venus 1* (which would operate until 1992) maps Venus's surface but discovers no magnetic field

NASA atmospheric probe *Pioneer Venus 2* studies clouds

Soviet orbiter and lander *Venera 11* and *Venera 12* study Venus's atmosphere and weather, detecting lightning

1982 Soviet orbiter and lander pairs *Venera 13* and *Venera 14* return first color images of surface and soil analysis

1983 Soviet orbiters *Venera 15* and *Venera 16* use radar to map Venus's surface

1980s Radio telescopes at Arecibo Observatory map Venus's surface

1985 Soviet lander and atmospheric probes *Vega 1* and *Vega 2* study planet's clouds, winds, and soil

1990 NASA probe *Galileo* flies by Venus on its way to Jupiter

NASA orbiter *Magellan* uses radar to penetrate Venus's thick clouds and map 99 percent of its surface

1998–1999 NASA probe *Cassini* makes two flybys of Venus on its way to Saturn

2006–2007 NASA probe *MESSENGER* makes two flybys of Venus on its way to Mercury

2006 European Space Agency orbiter *Venus Express* begins its three-year study of Venus (www.esa.int/science/venusexpress)

2011 Japanese orbiter *Planet-C* to arrive at Venus after 2010 launch (www.jaxa.jp/projects/sat/planet_c/index_e.html)

Earth

Symbol:

Color: blue

Moons: 1 (Luna)

Rings: none

Diameter: 7,926 miles (12,756 km)

Mass: 13,170,000,000,000 trillion pounds
(5,973,700,000,000 trillion kg)

Gravity: an 85-pound (38.5-kg) kid weighs 85 pounds
(38.5 kg)

Position: third planet from Sun

Distance from Sun: 93 million miles (150 million km)

Rotation (Day Length): 24 hours

Orbit (Year Length): 365 Earth days

Atmosphere: 78 percent nitrogen, 21 percent oxygen;
1 percent trace amounts of argon, carbon dioxide,
and water vapor

Surface: rock and water

Minimum/Maximum Temperature: -126°F /136°F
(-88°C /58°C)

WHAT'S IT LIKE?

Earth is a terrestrial planet made of rock. But nearly
three-quarters of its surface is covered in liquid
water, thanks to mild temperatures. Earth's land is
covered in mountains, volcanoes, deserts, oceans,
ice, and freshwater lakes and rivers. The air is mostly
nitrogen and oxygen, with traces of carbon dioxide,
water vapor, and argon. Earth spins at a tilt. That
means that different places get more sunlight during
parts of the year, creating seasons. There are all
kinds of life forms on Earth living in the air and
water, and on land.

EARTHLY FACTS

- Earth is the only place in the solar system
  where life as been found—so far! Life's been
  here for at least 3.9 billion years.

- Earth is geologically alive, too. Every 500 million
  years or so, erosion and movements of the plates
  that make up the Earth's crust erase and recycle
  most of the Earth's surface.

- The center, or core, of the Earth is liquid metal.
  Its temperature is hotter than that of the surface
  of the Sun.

- The oxygen in Earth's atmosphere comes from
  plants. Without life there would be no oxygen
  in the air.

- Earth is the fifth largest planet in the solar system.

- The Moon slows the Earth's spin by about 2 milli-
  seconds per century. About 900 million years ago
  there were 481 18-hour days in a year, instead of
  365 24-hour days.

- The blue color of Earth's sky is created by water
  droplets in the air.

- Earth's rapid spin and molten nickel-iron core
  create a magnetic field around the planet.

- When solar wind particles are trapped in Earth's
  magnetic field and crash into air molecules
  above the magnetic poles, the air molecules glow
  and create the auroras, or the Northern and
  Southern Lights.

- Earth is the only planet that does not get its name
  from Greek or Roman mythology. The Greek name
  for Mother Earth is Gaia; the Roman goddess of
  Earth was Tellus.

EARTH EXPLORATION TIME LINE

200 B.C. Eratosthenes uses shadows to determine that the radius of the Earth is about 3,840 miles (6,400 km)

A.D. 140 Ptolemy proposes that Earth is the center of the cosmos

1543 Copernicus states that the Earth is one of the planets that orbit the Sun

1957 Soviet satellite *Sputnik 1* is the first satellite to orbit Earth

Soviet satellite *Sputnik 2* carries a dog into orbit

United States' Vanguard TV3 fails to launch when its rocket explodes on the launch pad

1958 *Explorer 1*, the United States' first successful satellite, discovers the Van Allen belt

Five U.S. Vanguard satellites fail to launch

Soviet satellite *Sputnik* fails

U.S. satellite *Explorer 2* fails to orbit

U.S. satellite *Vanguard 1* discovers the Earth's pear shape

U.S. satellite *Explorer 3* collects radiation and micrometeoroid data

Soviet satellite *Sputnik 3* orbits Earth

U.S. satellite *Explorer 4* maps Van Allen belt for 2 ½ months

U.S. satellite *Explorer 5* fails to orbit

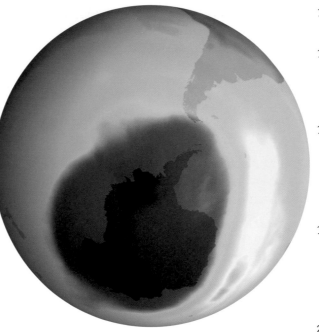

This Earth-orbiting satellite image shows the ozone hole in blue.

1960 NASA's *Television Infrared Observation Satellite* (*TIROS*) is the first weather satellite. (Thousands of earth-orbiting satellites have been launched since.)

1968 United States' Geostationary Operational Environmental Satellites (GOES) program begins

1972 United States' Landsat satellite series begins to observe land surface

1990 NASA probe *Galileo* makes its first Earth flyby on the way to Jupiter

1991 NASA's *Upper Atmosphere Research Satellite* (*UARS*), the first satellite in the Mission to Planet Earth program, provides evidence that human-made chemicals cause the ozone hole

1992 *TOPEX/Poseidon*, a U.S./French satellite, maps ocean surface and studies links between oceans and climate

Galileo makes its second flyby on the way to Jupiter

1999 *Terra*, NASA's Earth Observing System (EOS) flagship satellite, measures the state of Earth's environment (http://terra.nasa.gov)

NASA satellite *Landsat 7* maps Earth's landmasses (http://landsat.gsfc.nasa.gov)

2000 NASA's Space Transport System, part of its Radar Topography mission, maps 80 percent of Earth's surface down to 98 feet (30 m) resolution

2002 NASA's *Aqua* satellite studies Earth's water cycle (http://aqua.nasa.gov)

2004 *Aura* takes measurements of the composition and chemistry of Earth's atmosphere (http://aura.gsfc.nasa.gov)

2008 Europe's *Gravity Field and Steady-State Ocean Circulation Explorer* (*GOCE*) satellite to measure Earth's gravity (www.esa.int/esaLP/LPgoce.html)

Moon

Symbol:

Color: gray

Rings: none

Diameter: 2,160 miles (3,476 km)

Mass: less than one-fiftieth (1.2 percent) of Earth's

Gravity: an 85 pound (38.5-kg) kid would weigh 14.5 pounds (6.5 kg)

Position: orbits third planet from Sun

Distance from Earth: 238,855 miles (384,400 km)

Rotation (Day Length): 648 hours

Orbit (Year Length) around Earth: 27 days

Atmosphere: none

Surface: rocks and dust

Minimum/Maximum Temperature: -387°F /253°F (-233°C /123°C)

WHAT'S IT LIKE?

The Moon is an airless, lifeless, gray world. Its surface is covered in gray powdery soil called lunar regolith. During the day it reaches a blistering 253°F (123°C)! But because there's no atmosphere to hold in that heat, the temperature drops into negative numbers each night once the Sun no longer shines directly on it. The lack of air also allows meteors and comets to hit the Moon at full speed. (In contrast, most meteors burn up in Earth's atmosphere before reaching its surface.) Many of the Moon's impact craters are millions of years old. They never erode because there's no wind or rain. And the crust of the Moon isn't recycled back into a molten layer, as the Earth's surface is. The dark and light areas on the Moon have inspired humans to imagine a "Man in the Moon" face there. The light areas are actually lunar highlands covered in regolith. The dark features are craters, called maria, that were filled with dark lava millions of years ago.

LUNAR FACTS

- The Moon both rotates and orbits in 27 days. This "synchronous rotation" means that the same side is always facing Earth.

- Humans have sent more than 70 spacecraft to the Moon, and 12 astronauts have walked on its surface.

- Astronauts have collected 842 pounds (382 kg) of rocks and soil from the Moon.

- Tides on Earth are caused by the Moon's gravitational pull on our planet. High tides occur on the side of the Earth that is facing the Moon.

- Where did the Moon come from? Scientists think that a Mars-sized *something* slammed into Earth about 4.5 billion years ago, and that the leftover debris formed the Moon.

- The Moon's Tycho Crater is more than 52 miles (85 km) wide! It was named after 16th-century astronomer Tycho Brahe.

- It would take more than 20 weeks to travel to the Moon at 70 miles (113 km) per hour.

MOON EXPLORATION TIME LINE

PREHISTORY Humans mark the passage of time by lunar phases and daily moonrises

circa 200 B.C. Ancient Chinese predict lunar eclipses

circa 150 B.C. Hipparchus explains the Moon's phases and uses parallax to estimate its distance

1610 Galileo Galilei sees craters and mountains on the Moon through his telescope.

1837 Wilhelm Beer and Johann Heinrich Mädler publish a detailed map of the Moon's near side and deduce from its unchanging, sharp shadows an absence of atmosphere

1840 First close-up photographs of the Moon are taken through a telescope

1930 Using a vacuum thermocouple device, Seth Nicholson measures the surface temperature of the Moon

1946 U.S. Army Signal Corps bounces radar signals off of the Moon, giving birth to radar astronomy

1950s Astronomers measure microwave radiation to determine lunar temperatures

1958 U.S. Air Force orbiter *Pioneer 0* explodes during launch

Pioneer 1, the first spacecraft launched by NASA, fails to reach the Moon

Pioneer 2 and *Pioneer 3* probes fail to reach the Moon

1959 Soviet probe *Luna 1* makes the first lunar flyby, but fails to impact as planned

NASA flyby probe *Pioneer 4* passes within 37,300 miles (60,030 km) of the Moon

Soviet lander *Luna 2* is the first spacecraft to impact the Moon

Soviet flyby probe *Luna 3* returns the first photographs of the Moon's far side

Pioneer P-3 fails to during launch

1961 NASA orbiters *Ranger 1* and *Ranger 2* fail to reach the Moon

1962 NASA lander *Ranger 3* fails to reach the Moon

NASA hard lander *Ranger 4* is the first U.S. spacecraft to impact the Moon

NASA lander *Ranger 5* becomes a flyby probe due to spacecraft's failure to land on the Moon

1963 Soviet probe *Sputnik 25* fails

Soviet lander *Luna 4* fails to reach the Moon

1964 NASA lunar probe *Ranger 6* impacts the Moon

NASA lander *Ranger 7* sends back the first close-ups of the Moon before impact

1965 NASA landers *Ranger 8* and *Ranger 9* send back high-resolution images of the Moon before impact

Soviet lander *Luna 5* fails to make a soft landing and crashes on the Moon

Soviet lander *Luna 6* fails to reach the Moon

Soviet flyby probe *Zond 3* sends back pictures of the Moon's far side

Soviet landers *Luna 7* and *Luna 8* fail to make soft landings and crash on the Moon

1966 Soviet lander *Luna 9* makes the first soft lunar landing and transmits the first images from the Moon's surface

Soviet probe *Cosmos 111* fails to reach the Moon

Green triangles represent NASA Apollo missions, yellow triangles represent NASA Surveyor missions, and red triangles represent Soviet Luna spacecraft.

Soviet orbiter *Luna 10* is the first spacecraft to orbit the Moon and to study its radiation, gravitation, and magnetic field

NASA lander *Surveyor 1* is the first soft-landing robotic laboratory

NASA orbiter *Lunar Orbiter 1* circles the Moon and photographs 2 million square miles (5,180,000 sq. km) of its surface, then impacts on command

Soviet orbiter *Luna 11* becomes a lunar satellite

NASA lander *Surveyor 2* fails to make a soft landing and crashes on the Moon

Soviet orbiter *Luna 12* orbits Moon and transmits pictures

NASA orbiter *Lunar Orbiter 2* circles the Moon and photographs potential Apollo landing sites, then impacts on command

Soviet lander *Luna 13* makes a soft landing and measures soil density and lunar radioactivity

1967 NASA orbiter *Lunar Orbiter 3* circles the Moon, photographs potential Apollo landing sites, then impacts on command

NASA lander *Surveyor 3* returns photographs and soil-sample data from its robotic laboratory

NASA lunar orbiter *Lunar Orbiter 4* provides the first pictures of the lunar south pole, then impacts on command

NASA lander *Surveyor 4* loses radio contact with Earth and crashes on the Moon

NASA orbiter *Explorer 35* circles the Moon and sends back interplanetary data through 1972

NASA orbiter *Lunar Orbiter 5* circles Moon, photographs sites, and impacts on command

NASA lander *Surveyor 5* sets its robotic laboratory down in the Sea of Tranquility

NASA lander *Surveyor 6* both lands on and takes off from the lunar surface

1968 NASA lander *Surveyor 7* sets its robotic laboratory down near Tycho Crater

Soviet orbiter *Luna 14* studies the lunar gravitational field

Soviet probe *Zond 5* is the first spacecraft to fly around Moon and return to Earth

Soviet probe *Zond 6* flies around the Moon and returns to Earth

NASA crewed orbiter *Apollo 8* carries the first humans around the Moon 10 times, then returns them to Earth

1969 NASA crewed orbiter *Apollo 10* makes the first docking maneuvers in lunar orbit and tests a piloted lunar landing to within 9.5 miles (15 km) of the Moon's surface

Soviet sample-return probe *Luna 15* fails and crashes during its landing on the Moon

NASA crewed lander *Apollo 11* sets down in the Sea of Tranquility and puts the first humans on the Moon

Soviet probe *Zond 7* flies around the Moon and returns to Earth

Soviet probes *Cosmos 300* and *Cosmos 305* fail to reach the Moon

NASA crewed lander *Apollo 12* carries astronauts to the Ocean of Storms area

1970 NASA crewed lander *Apollo 13* fails to reach the Moon, but astronauts safely return to Earth

Soviet sample-return probe *Luna 16* lands the first robotic return vehicle, which brings four ounces (100 g) of lunar samples back to Earth

Soviet flyby probe *Zond 8* circles the Moon and returns to Earth

Soviet lander *Luna 17* carries *Lunokhod 1*, the first robotic rover, to the Moon

1971 NASA crewed lander *Apollo 14* carries astronauts to the Moon's Fra Mauro highlands, where they collect rock and soil samples

NASA crewed lander *Apollo 15* carries astronauts to the Moon's Hadley-Apennine area

Soviet sample-return probe *Luna 18* fails and crashes during its landing on the Moon

Soviet orbiter *Luna 19* studies the Moon's gravitational field through 1972

1972 Soviet sample-return probe *Luna 20* lands and returns one ounce (30 g) of lunar samples to Earth

NASA crewed lander *Apollo 16* sets astronauts down in the Descartes Crater

Apollo 17, NASA's final crewed Apollo lander, carries astronauts to the Moon's Taurus-Littrow Valley

1973 Soviet lander *Luna 21* sets the robotic *Lunokhod 2* rover on the Moon

1974 Soviet orbiter *Luna 22* successfully orbits the Moon through 1975

Soviet sample-return probe *Luna 23* lands on the Moon but fails to leave its surface

1976 Soviet sample-return probe *Luna 24* lands on the Moon and returns collected moon rocks to Earth

1990 Japanese orbiters *Hiten* make Japan the third nation to reach the Moon

Galileo flies by the Moon on its way to Jupiter

1994 NASA orbiter *Clementine* creates the first topographic lunar map

1998 NASA orbiter *Lunar Prospector* discovers water-based ice at the Moon's poles and maps lunar resources, gravity, and magnetic fields

2004 European orbiter *SMART 1* orbits and maps the Moon

2007 Japan's SELenological and ENgineering Explorer (SELENE) mission's orbiter maps the Moon's surface and studies lunar origins (http://selene.tksc.jaxa.jp/en/index.htm)

2008 *Lunar Reconnaissance Orbiter*, the first mission of NASA's Robotic Lunar Exploration Program, to search for future crewed lunar mission landing sites (http://lunar.gsfc.nasa.gov)

Mars ♂

Symbol:

Color: rust

Moons: 2 (Phobos, Deimos)

Rings: none

Diameter: 4,222 miles (6,794 km)

Mass: about one-tenth (11 percent) that of Earth's

Gravity: an 85-pound (38.5-kg) kid would weigh 32 pounds (15 kg)

Position: fourth planet from Sun

Distance from Sun: 142 million miles (228 million km)

Rotation (Day Length): 24 hours, 37 minutes

Orbit (Year Length): 687 Earth days

Atmosphere: 95 percent carbon dioxide; 3 percent nitrogen; 2 percent argon

Surface: rock

Minimum/Maximum Temperature: -125°F /23°F (-87°C /-5°C)

WHAT'S IT LIKE?

Mars is a cold desert—even daytime temperatures remain below freezing. Nights are even chillier, with temperatures reaching down into three-digit negative numbers in some places. Mars's thin atmosphere is mostly made up of the stuff we exhale—carbon dioxide. Like Earth, Mars is tilted, so it has seasons.

Summer's warming often brings planet-wide dust storms, while winter creates carbon-dioxide frost. Mars is a rocky planet with huge canyons and boulder-strewn plains. There are also volcanoes and polar ice caps on Mars. Martian soil is sandy and red from iron oxide, or rust. The red dust in the air makes the sky pink. The southern hemisphere of Mars is mostly Moon-like, ancient cratered highlands. The northern hemisphere is younger plains.

MARTIAN FACTS

- Mars's two small moons, Phobos and Deimos, are each less than 17 miles (27 km) across, and both are kind of potato-shaped.

- Olympus Mons, a huge inactive volcano that is three times the size of Mt. Everest, is likely the biggest volcano in the solar system.

- Valles Marineris is an enormous canyon that is nearly as long as the United States is wide.

- Spring, summer, autumn, and winter last twice as long as these seasons do on Earth.

- There's no liquid water on Mars now. But scientists think that Mars had big floods billions of years ago. There's still lots of frozen water below the surface, near the poles.

- Because there are no oceans on Mars, the amount of land surface area on Mars is about the same as Earth's.

- Mars's moons Phobos and Deimos probably used to be asteroids until they were caught by Mars's gravity.

- Mars is one of the brightest objects in the night sky, and its reddish light earned it the name the Red Planet.

- Mars was named after the Roman god of war, and it shares the symbol for male.

MARS EXPLORATION TIME LINE

PREHISTORY Humans observe its movements across the night sky

1609 Johannes Kepler discovers its elliptical orbit

1610 Galileo Galilei observes Mars through a telescope

1659 Christiaan Huygens makes first accurate drawings of Mars

1666 Giovanni Cassini discovers its polar ice caps and measures Mars's rotation

1790s William Herschel notes Mars's thin atmosphere and measures its season-creating tilt

1877 Asaph Hall discovers Phobos and Deimos

1878 Giovanni Schiaparelli claims to see a system of canals on Mars

1960 Soviet flyby probes *Marsnik 1* and *Marsnik 2* both fail to reach Earth orbit

1962 Soviet flyby probes and Soviet lander *Sputnik 24* break apart in Earth orbit

1964 NASA flyby probe *Mariner 3* fails to reach Mars

Contact with Soviet flyby probe *Zond 2* lost during its voyage to Mars

1965 NASA flyby probe *Mariner 4*, the first spacecraft to fly by Mars, takes pictures as it passes within 6,117 miles (9,844 km) of the planet and confirms the thin carbon dioxide atmosphere

1969 NASA flyby probes *Mariner 6* and *Mariner 7* pass within 2,131 miles (3,430 km) of Mars's surface; send back images; help establish the mass, radius, and shape of the planet; and show that the southern polar ice cap is carbon dioxide ice, not frozen water

Mars 1969A and *Mars 1969B* fail to launch

1971 NASA flyby probe *Mariner 8* fails to reach Earth orbit

Soviet orbiter *Cosmos 419* launches, then fails and reenters Earth's atmosphere

Soviet probes *Mars 2* and *Mars 3* each orbit Mars and release a lander to map the planet's surface and record temperatures, gravity, and magnetic fields (*Mars 2*'s lander crashed)

NASA orbiter *Mariner 9*, the first spacecraft to orbit another planet, takes 7,329 images, studies Mars's surface and the density and pressure of its atmosphere, and provides a first look at its two moons

1974 Soviet orbiter *Mars 4* becomes a flyby probe when retro-rockets fail

Soviet orbiter *Mars 5* completes 22 orbits and returns 60 images

Soviet probes *Mars 6* and *Mars 7* fail to collect data

1976 NASA orbiter-lander probes *Viking 1* and *Viking 2* put orbiters around Mars and successfully set landers on its surface, taking weather readings and thousands of color images as well as sampling soil for signs of microscopic life

1988   Soviet orbiter-lander *Phobos 1* fails to reach Mars

1989   Soviet orbiter-lander *Phobos 2* reaches Mars's orbit but loses contact with Earth before landing on Phobos

1993   NASA orbiter *Mars Observer* loses contact with Mission Control en route to Mars

1996   Russian orbiter-lander *Mars '96*, carrying two soil-penetrating devices, crashes back to Earth when its rocket's fourth stage fails

Scientist David McKay identifies what seem like microscopic fossils in a Martian meteorite found in Antarctica

1997   NASA orbiter *Mars Global Surveyor* begins returning images and data from Mars

NASA lander *Mars Pathfinder* and its rover, *Sojourner*, collect weather data, take images, and analyze rocks in the Ares Vallis region

1999   NASA's *Mars Climate Orbiter* burns up in Mars's atmosphere after being sent commands that were not in metric units

Contact is lost with NASA's *Mars Polar Lander* and *Deep Space 2* probes

2001   NASA orbiter *Mars Odyssey* begins mapping the planet's surface

2003   *Mars Express*, the first European probe to visit

another planet, begins orbiting Mars (www.sci.esa.int/marsexpress); however, contact is lost with its lander, *Beagle 2*

Japanese orbiter *Nozomi* fails to orbit Mars

2004   NASA's twin Mars Exploration Rovers (MER), *Spirit* and *Opportunity*, study the geology of Mars with robotic arms, a drilling tool, three spectrometers, and four pairs of cameras and discover evidence of ancient surface water (http://marsrovers.nasa.gov)

2006   NASA's *Mars Reconnaissance Orbiter* begins scanning for water on Mars (http://mars.jpl.nasa.gov/mro)

2008   NASA Mars Scout mission lander *Phoenix* to set down on Mars (http://phoenix.lpl.arizona.edu)

2010   NASA's *Mars Science Laboratory* rover to begin a two-year search for life after a 2009 launch (http://mars.jpl.nasa.gov/msl)

2012   NASA probe *Mars Scout* to arrive after a 2011 launch (http://mars.jpl.nasa.gov/missions/future/2005-plus.html)

2014   NASA's *Mars Sample-Return Lander* to return soil and rocks collected on Mars to Earth after a three-year mission (http://mars.jpl.nasa.gov/missions/future/futureMissions.html)

Jupiter

Symbol:
Color: orange with stripes
Moons: 63
Rings: 4
Diameter: 88,846 miles (142,984 km)
Mass: equal to about 318 Earths
Gravity: an 85-pound (38.5-kg) kid would weigh 201 pounds (91 kg)
Position: fifth planet from Sun
Distance from Sun: 484 million miles (778 million km)
Rotation (Day Length): 9 hours, 55 minutes
Orbit (Year Length): 4,331 Earth days
Atmosphere: 90 percent hydrogen; 10 percent helium
Surface: none
Average Temperature: -234°F (-148°C)

WHAT'S IT LIKE?

Jupiter is so big and has so many moons that it's like a mini solar system. Its colored stripes and swirls are actually icy, windswept clouds made of ammonia and water that float above a poisonous atmosphere of helium and hydrogen. There is no land on Jupiter. Like all gas giant planets, Jupiter is a spinning ball of gas with a super-hot liquid center that is under incredible pressure. Jupiter's largest moons are more like terrestrial planets. In fact, Ganymede is larger than Pluto and Mercury. Europa probably has an ocean under its icy surface, and Io has more volcanoes than any other moon—or any planet.

JOVIAN FACTS

- Spaceships will never land on Jupiter—there's no land! Even if there was land, the pressure of Jupiter's thick gases would crush a spacecraft.

- The Great Red Spot is a permanent hurricane that is as wide as three Earths.

- Jupiter is so huge that more than 1,300 Earths could fit inside it.

- If Jupiter had been between 50 and 100 times more massive, it would have become a star.

- It takes a dozen Earth years for Jupiter to travel around the Sun once.

- What appears to be a faint ring around Jupiter is actually four separate thin rings.

- The four large moons discovered by Galileo Galilei in 1610—Callisto, Europa, Ganymede, and Io—are known as the Galilean satellites.

- Ganymede is the solar system's largest moon.

- Many of Jupiter's small outer moons are probably asteroids that have been captured by the planet's gravity.

- Astronomers witnessed a spectacular event in July 1994, when 21 fragments of a comet named Shoemaker-Levy 9 crashed into Jupiter's atmosphere.

The impacts caused tremendous explosions, some of which scattered debris over areas that are larger than the diameter of Earth.

- Jupiter was named after the Roman king of the gods.

JUPITER EXPLORATION TIME LINE

PREHISTORY Humans observe Jupiter's movements across the night sky

1610 Galileo Galilei discovers Callisto, Europa, Ganymede, and Io

1655 Giovanni Cassini discovers Jupiter's Great Red Spot

1665 Giovanni Cassini determines the length of a day on Jupiter

1892 Astronomer Edward Barnard discovers one of Jupiter's moons, which is later named Amalthea

1973 NASA flyby probe *Pioneer 10* is the first spacecraft to pass through the asteroid belt and to fly within 124,000 miles (200,000 km) of Jupiter's clouds; it studies the planet's magnetic field and atmosphere and takes the first close-up pictures of Jupiter

1974 NASA flyby probe *Pioneer 11* flies by Jupiter, comes within 21,100 miles (34,000 km) of the planet's cloud tops, studies its magnetic field and atmosphere, and takes pictures of Jupiter and some of its moons

1979 NASA flyby probes *Voyager 1* and *Voyager 2* pass by the Jovian system, snapping 18,000 images of Jupiter and its moons and discovering three new moons, active volcanoes on Io, and a thin, dark ring (later determined to be four rings) around Jupiter

1992 NASA orbiter *Ulysses*, on its way to study the Sun, flies by and gets a gravity assist

1994 *Galileo* (en route to Jupiter), the *Hubble Space Telescope*, and Earth-based telescopes view comet Shoemaker-Levy 9 crash into Jupiter's atmosphere

1995 *Galileo* goes into orbit a day after its atmospheric probe is released toward Jupiter, sending back weather information before being crushed by the planet's pressure. *Galileo* relays the atmospheric probe's data and then takes images of Jupiter and the larger moons through 2003, uncovering evidence of liquid-water oceans under Europa's ice

2000 NASA probe *Cassini* flies by and takes pictures of Jupiter on its way to Saturn

2003 Using huge digital cameras mounted on powerful telescopes atop Hawaii's Mauna Kea volcano, astronomers discover 23 new moons surrounding Jupiter

2007 NASA probe *New Horizons* flies by Jupiter on its way to Pluto, studying and photographing the giant planet, its ring, and moons

2016 NASA *Jupiter Polar Orbiter* (*Juno*) to arrive at Jupiter after a 2011 launch (http://juno.wisc.edu)

Saturn

Symbol:

Color: yellow

Moons: 60

Rings: 7

Diameter: 74,898 miles (120,536 km)

Mass: equal to about 95 Earths

Gravity: an 85-pound (38.5-kg) kid would weigh 77 pounds (35 kg)

Position: sixth planet from Sun

Distance from Sun: 886 million miles (1,427 million km)

Rotation (Day Length): 10 hours 39 minutes

Orbit (Year Length): 10,756 Earth days

Atmosphere: 97 percent hydrogen; 3 percent helium

Surface: none

Temperature: -288°F (-178°C)

WHAT'S IT LIKE?

Like other gas giant planets, Saturn has no solid land. It's a swirling ball of gas and high-pressure liquid. Winds around its equator reach speeds of 1,118 miles (1,800 km) per hour—five times faster than the most violent Earth tornado! Thin clouds of water and ammonia stream above cold hydrogen and helium, giving Saturn its yellow and gold bands of color. Saturn has the most complex system of rings in the

solar system. The rings extend many thousands of miles away from the planet and are less than one kilometer (.62 mile) thick. Saturn's largest moon, Titan, is bigger than Mercury, and it has an atmosphere that is similar to ancient Earth's.

SATURNIAN FACTS

• Saturn's ring system is made up of billions of bits of ice, dust, and rock.

• Some ring particles are as small as a grain of sugar, while others are as big as a house.

- The entire planet and all its rings would just fit between the Earth and the Moon.

- The *Cassini* spacecraft successfully flew through the gap between two of the major rings.

- When Galileo Galilei spotted Saturn's rings in 1610, he didn't know what planetary rings were. He believed he was seeing a triple planet—a big Saturn with two smaller planets on either side of it.

- Saturn is the least dense of all the planets— it would float in water.

- It's the farthest planet you can see without a telescope.

- The word Saturday comes from the word Saturn.

- Saturn was named for the Roman god of agriculture.

The *Huygens* probe is readied for its attachment to *Cassini*.

SATURN EXPLORATION TIME LINE

PREHISTORY Humans observe Saturn's movements across the night sky

1610 Galileo Galilei sees Saturn's rings, but doesn't know what they are

1650s Christiaan Huygens identifies Saturn's rings as rings; discovers Titan

1671–1672 Giovanni Cassini discovers Iapetus and Rhea

1675 Giovanni Cassini discovers a gap in two of Saturn's rings, which is later named the Cassini Division

1684 Giovanni Cassini discovers Dione and Tethys

1789 William Herschel discovers Mimas and Enceladus

1848 Astronomers William and George Bond and astronomer William Lassell discover Hyperion

1850 William and George Bond and astronomer William Rutter Dawes discover inner ring of Saturn

1856 Physicist James Clerk Maxwell argues that Saturn's rings consist of a many tiny satellites, stating that a solid ring would be torn apart by gravity

1898 William Pickering discovers Phoebe

1944 Gerard Kuiper discovers Titan's atmosphere

1979 NASA flyby probe *Pioneer 11* is first to visit Saturn, passing within 13,000 miles (21,000 km) of its cloud tops, studying its atmosphere, icy rings, and magnetic field, and taking pictures of the planet and some of its moons

1980–1981 NASA flyby probes *Voyager 1* and *Voyager 2* pass by the planet's cloud tops, take almost 16,000 images, and discover three new moons, the structure of the ring system, and information about the planet's atmosphere and magnetic field

1990 NASA's orbiting *Hubble Space Telescope* observes a giant storm that is later named the Great White Spot

2004 NASA orbiter *Cassini* begins its four-year orbit around Saturn, which takes it by many of the planet's moons (http://saturn.jpl.nasa.gov)

2005 European probe *Huygens* (released from *Cassini*) studies Titan's atmosphere as it descends. Then it lands on Titan, sending back pictures and data from the surface for a few hours (http://huygens.esa.int)

Uranus

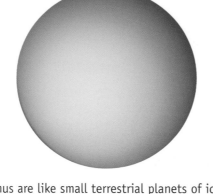

Symbol:

Color: blue-green

Moons: 27

Rings: 13

Diameter: 31,764 miles (51,118 km)

Mass: equal to about 14 Earths

Gravity: an 85-pound (38.5-kg) kid would weigh 76 pounds (34 kg)

Position: seventh planet from Sun

Distance from Sun: 1,784 million miles (2,871 million km)

Rotation (Day Length): 17 hours 14 minutes

Orbit (Year Length): 30,687 Earth days

Atmosphere: 83 percent hydrogen; 15 percent helium; 2 percent methane

Surface: none

Temperature: -357°F (-216°C)

WHAT'S IT LIKE?

Uranus is a cold, windy world made of gases and liquid. There is no land. Its poisonous atmosphere is topped with bright blue-green clouds of frozen methane (natural gas) crystals. Deeper inside the planet, it gets very hot. A deep, superheated layer of water, ammonia, and methane boils and bubbles up gases that form into clouds. The larger moons of Uranus are like small terrestrial planets of ice and rock. The odd moon Miranda has high cliffs and winding valleys.

URANIAN FACTS

- Uranus lies almost on its side, which means its poles get more sunlight than does its equator. Scientists speculate that the planet might have been knocked over when it crashed into something long ago.

- Each season on Uranus lasts more than 20 Earth years.

- Uranus is pronounced YUR-un-nus, not "yur-AY-nus" or "YU-rin-us"

- Its thin and dark rings might be broken-up moons.

- When English astronomer William Herschel first saw Uranus, he thought it was a comet.

- It was the first planet that was discovered through the use of a telescope.

- Its many moons are named after characters in plays by William Shakespeare and poems of Alexander Pope.

This false-color image of Uranus, taken by the *Hubble Space Telescope*, shows the planet's four major rings and ten of its moons.

- It's the third largest planet in the solar system.
- Uranus was named for the Roman god who was the father of the Titans.

URANUS EXPLORATION TIME LINE

1781　Using a telescope, William Herschel discovers Uranus

1787　William Herschel discovers Titania and Oberon

1851　William Lassell discovers Ariel and Umbriel

1932　Using spectroscopy, scientist Rupert Wildt detects methane in Uranus's atmosphere

1948　Gerard Kuiper discovers Miranda

1952　Scientist Gerhard Herzberg detects hydrogen in Uranus's atmosphere

1977　Using radar while on board the Kuiper Airborne Observatory, James Elliot discovers Uranus's rings

1986　NASA flyby probe *Voyager 2* becomes the first (and only, so far) spacecraft to visit Uranus, coming within 50,600 miles (81,500 km) of the planet's cloud tops, taking almost 8,000 images of the planet, studying its dark ring system, and discovering 10 new moons

1990s　NASA's *Hubble Space Telescope* observes the planet's atmosphere and clouds

2003　*Hubble Space Telescope* discovers two small moons

Neptune ♆

Symbol:

Color: blue

Moons: 13

Rings: 6

Diameter: 30,776 miles (49,528 km)

Mass: equal to about 17 Earths

Gravity: an 85-pound (38.5-kg) kid would weigh 95 pounds (43 kg)

Position: eighth planet from Sun

Distance from Sun: 2,795 million miles (4,498 million km)

Rotation (Day Length): 16 hours 7 minutes

Orbit (Year Length): 60,190 Earth days

Atmosphere: 79 percent hydrogen; 18 percent helium; 3 percent methane

Surface: none

Temperature: -353°F (-214°C)

WHAT'S IT LIKE?

Neptune is a cold, distant world and the farthest planet. In fact, it's even farther from the Sun than Pluto during 20 years of Pluto's 248-year, slanted orbit. There's no land on Neptune, but winds whip through the blue methane clouds at more than 1,200 miles (2,000 km) per hour. An atmosphere of hydrogen and helium floats above a planet-wide ocean of

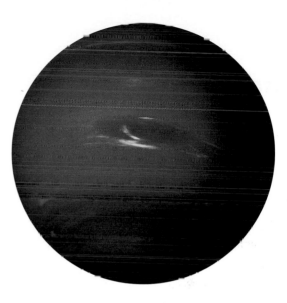

superhot, highly pressurized water. Its largest moon, Triton, is even colder than Pluto, and has great geysers that spew out nitrogen gas.

NEPTUNIAN FACTS

- It's the smallest of the four gas giants, but it would still hold the volume of nearly 60 Earths.
- It hasn't made a complete orbit around the Sun since it was discovered.
- Triton orbits Neptune in the opposite direction of the planet's spin, and the moon is slowly getting closer. Eventually (in 10 to 100 million years) it will collide with the planet and break up into a ring system that is bigger than Saturn's.
- With surface temperatures that reach down to -391°F (-235°C), Triton is the coldest body in our solar system yet visited.

- Neptune's Great Dark Spot is a huge storm that is the size of Earth.

- Neptune was the first planet located through the use of a mathematical prediction instead of by observation of the night sky.

- Neptune was named after the Roman god of the sea.

NEPTUNE EXPLORATION TIME LINE

1845 Mathematicians John Adams and Urbain Leverrier independently predict the existence and location of Neptune from irregularities in the orbit of Uranus

1846 Astronomer Johann Galle discovers Neptune

1846 William Lassell discovers Triton

1949 Gerard Kuiper discovers Nereid

1952 Gerhard Herzberg detects hydrogen in Neptune's atmosphere

1985 Astronomers on Earth discover rings around Neptune

1989 NASA flyby probe *Voyager 2* becomes the first (and only, so far) spacecraft to reach Neptune, flying within 5,000 kilometers (3,105 miles) of the planet's cloud tops, returning 10,000 images of Neptune and its moons and ring system, and discovering six additional moons

1998 *Hubble Space Telescope* observes changes in Neptune's atmosphere

Pluto

Dwarf Planets

Color: varies

Moons: sometimes

Rings: none known

Diameter: at least 500 miles (800 km)

Mass: at least enough to force a round shape, about one ten-thousandth (.01 percent) of Earth's

Gravity: an 85-pound (38.5-kg) kid would weigh about 7 pounds (3 kg) on Pluto, 2.5 pounds (1.1 kg) on Ceres

Position: varies

Distance from Sun: varies

Atmosphere: varies

Surface: rock and/or ice

Minimum/Maximum Temperature: varies

WHAT ARE THEY LIKE?

Dwarf planets are a new category of space objects. The International Astronomical Union (IAU) defines a dwarf planet as an object that orbits the Sun, is large enough for gravity to force it into a sphere, has not cleared other things out of its orbital neighborhood, and is not a moon. The three official dwarf planets so far—Eris, Pluto, and Ceres—are small worlds made of rock and ice with little atmosphere. They share their orbits with lots of smaller objects, like asteroids or KBOs.

CERES FACTS

- When Ceres was discovered in 1801 it was called a planet. But as other objects near it were discovered, Ceres was reclassified as an asteroid for the next 150 years. Because it's large and round, it's now been reclassified again as a dwarf planet.

- Ceres likely has a rocky inner core, an icy mantle, and a thin, dusty outer crust. It might have a thin atmosphere, and its average surface temperature is -159°F (-106°C).

- Its day lasts only nine hours, but a year is more than 1,675 days due to its position between Mars and Jupiter.

- There's a large dark spot on Ceres that might be a crater.

- With a diameter of 590 miles (950 km), Ceres is the largest object by far in the asteroid belt. It alone makes up about a third of the belt's total mass.

PLUTO FACTS

- At a distance of 3,670 million miles (5,906 million km), the Sun is so far away that it looks like a bright star in Pluto's continually dark sky.

- So little solar radiation reaches Pluto that it's cold enough there to freeze the air! Average temperature is about -356°F (-215°C).

- It has a solid, rocky surface that is covered with

nitrogen frost, methane, and carbon monoxide-based ice.

- Its diameter of 1,430 miles (2,302 km) means it's about two-thirds the size of Earth's moon.

- Pluto is part of the Kuiper belt, a band of billions of chunks and spheres of ice and rock (called Kuiper belt objects, or KBOs) that are located past Neptune.

- You'd never live long enough to have a birthday on Pluto—it takes 90,553 Earth days for a year to pass. Day length is 153 hours and 18 minutes.

- Largest moon Charon is about half Pluto's size. Its other two moons, Nix and Hydra, are tiny.

- Pluto's atmosphere is mostly nitrogen gas, with some carbon monoxide and methane.

- Pluto was named after the Roman god of the underworld.

ERIS FACTS

- With a diameter of about 1,850 miles (3,000 km), Eris is the largest dwarf planet in our solar system and the largest orbiting space object discovered since Neptune in 1846.

- Its surface is methane ice and has a temperature around -406°F (-243°C).

- Because it's nearly 10 billion miles (16 billion km) from the Sun, one orbit (or year length) takes 203,305 Earth days.

- Eris (pronounced EE-ris) was named after the Greek goddess of discord and strife. Its tiny moon is Dysnomia.

DWARF PLANET EXPLORATION TIME LINE

1801 Giuseppe Piazzi is the first to discover an asteroid, which is named Ceres

1905 Percival Lowell predicts the existence of "a ninth planet" and begins searching for it

1930 Clyde Tombaugh discovers Pluto

1955 Astronomers discover that Pluto's day length is 153 hours

1976 Astronomers discover methane on Pluto's surface

1978 Astronomers James Christy and Robert Harrington discover Charon

1988 Astronomers discover Pluto's atmosphere

1992 Astronomers discover nitrogen and carbon monoxide on Pluto's surface

1994 *Hubble Space Telescope* creates the first maps of Pluto

2002 Mike Brown and Chad Trujillo discover Quaoar

   Hubble Space Telescope photographs Quaoar

2003 Mike Brown discovers Sedna

2003–2004 *Hubble Space Telescope* takes close-up images of Ceres

2004 *Hubble Space Telescope* photographs Sedna

2005 Mike Brown discovers Eris and its moon Dysnomia

   Astronomers discover two additional small moons circling Pluto, Nix and Hydra

2006 IAU declares Pluto, Eris, and Ceres dwarf planets

2015 NASA orbiter *Dawn*, launched in 2007, to arrive at Ceres (http://dawn.jpl. nasa.gov)

2015 NASA probe *New Horizons*, launched in 2006, to become the first spacecraft to reach Pluto and the Kuiper belt (http://pluto.jhuapl.edu)

Comets

Diameter of nucleus: 1–50 miles (1.5–80 km)

Gravity: an 85-pound (38.5-kg) kid would weigh .16 ounces (4.5 g)

Orbit (Year Length): 75 to 30,000,000 Earth years

Atmosphere of coma: ammonia, carbon dioxide, carbon monoxide, and methane

Surface: rock and ice

WHAT ARE THEY LIKE?

A comet is a "dirty snowball" of ice and rock orbiting the Sun. Only a small part of a comet is its solid nucleus. The nucleus is made up of icy chunks and frozen gases covered in a crust of rock and dust. When a comet nears the Sun, it begins to warm up and its ice starts to evaporate, which creates holes in its crust. The stream of evaporating gases creates an atmosphere called a coma. It's the reflection of sunlight off this cloud of evaporating gases that we see from Earth. The solar wind blows the coma away from the comet, creating the comet's long, bright tail. A comet's tail always points away from the Sun.

COMET FACTS

- Comets are chunks of ice and rock left over from when the solar system formed about 4.6 billion years ago. Because they've hardly changed since then, they give us a peek into our solar system's past!

- Short-period comets take fewer than 200 years to orbit the Sun. Most come from the Kuiper belt, which lies beyond the orbit of Neptune. The Kuiper belt is full of icy celestial bodies called Kuiper belt objects (KBOs).

- Comets with orbits of more than 200 years are called long-period comets. These comets can take as many as 30 million years to circle around the Sun. Many long-period comets come from the Oort cloud.

- The Oort cloud, which is 100,000 times farther away than the distance between the Earth and the Sun, may be home to as many as a trillion long-period comets.

- Early Earth was probably hit by many comets, some of which deposited water and organic molecules here.

- About a dozen new comets are discovered each year.

- Sungrazers are comets that crash into the Sun or that travel so close to it that they vaporize.

- The word comet comes from the Latin word *cometa*. It means "long haired," as in "a long-haired star."

COMET EXPLORATION TIME LINE

PREHISTORY Humans observe comets' sudden appearances in the night sky

1059 B.C. Chinese court astrologer records a comet sighting

240 B.C. Chinese astronomers record seeing what would later be named Halley's comet

1577 Tycho Brahe uses parallax to prove that comets are distant objects

1618 Astronomers Johann Baptist Cysat and John Bainbridge are the first to use a telescope to observe a comet

1705 Edmond Halley predicts that a comet will appear in 53 years

1758 Halley's comet appears

1858 William Usherwood takes the first photograph of a comet

1864 Comet Tempel is the first comet analyzed with a spectroscope

1866 Giovanni Schiaparelli discovers that meteors are caused by the Earth passing through the orbit of a comet

1950 Scientist Jan Oort suggests that comets come from the Oort cloud

1951 Gerard Kuiper suggests that comets come from the Kuiper belt

1985 NASA's *ICE* is the first spacecraft to visit a comet, Giacobini-Zinner

1986 Soviet probes *Vega 1* and *Vega 2* make Halley flyby

Japanese probes *Sakigake* and *Suisei* make Halley flybys

European probes *Giotto* makes the closest Halley flyby to date

1992 European probe *Giotto* makes a flyby of comet Grigg-Skjellerup

1994 *Hubble Space Telescope* photographs comet Shoemaker-Levy 9's impact with Jupiter

NASA Jupiter orbiter *Galileo* observes Shoemaker-Levy 9's impact

1996 NASA's *Near Earth Asteroid Rendezvous* (*NEAR*) space probe studies comet Hyakutake on its way to asteroid Eros

NASA solar orbiter *Ulysses* unexpectedly encounters the longer-than-expected tail of Hyakutake

1997 Earthlings everywhere see Hale-Bopp with the naked eye

2001 NASA's *Deep Space 1* (*DS1*) probe flies by Borrelly

2002 NASA loses contact with its *Comet Nucleus Tour* (*CONTOUR*) spacecraft, ending the craft's mission to make flybys of comets Encke and Schwassmann-Wachmann 3

2005 NASA flyby probe *Deep Impact* successfully releases its impactor probe into Tempel 1 and studies what's ejected

2006 NASA sample-return probe *Stardust* delivers collected comet tail particles from Wild 2 to Earth (http://stardust.jpl.nasa.gov)

2014 European lander *Rosetta*, launched in 2004, to become the first to land on a comet as it sets down on Churymov-Gerasimenko (http://rosetta.esa.int)

Asteroids

Color: reddish or dark gray

Moons: sometimes

Rings: none

Diameter: 0.5–564 miles (1–940 km)

Mass: the mass of all of the asteroids combined is less than that of the Moon

Gravity: an 85-pound (38.5-kg) kid would weigh .8 ounces (20 g) on asteroid Mathilde

Position: most are located between Mars and Jupiter

Distance from Sun (asteroid belt): 186–273 million miles (300–600 million km)

Rotation (Day Length): 5–10 hours (larger asteroids)

Orbit (Year Length): approximately 600–2,000 Earth days

Atmosphere: none

Surface: rock

WHAT ARE THEY LIKE?

Asteroids are large space rocks orbiting the Sun. Made of stone and metals, they are like small, odd-shaped moons. Asteroid sizes range from about a quarter of the Moon's size to less than a half mile (1 km) across. Most of the millions of asteroids in the solar system are in the asteroid belt between Mars and Jupiter. Sometimes they get knocked out of this orbit and can slam into planets or moons—including Earth. The extinction of the dinosaurs was probably caused by changes in the climate that occurred when an asteroid hit Earth 65 million years ago.

ASTEROIDAL FACTS

- Asteroids are leftover rock chunks from when the solar system formed about 4.6 billion years ago. That's why they're so interesting!

- Hundreds of asteroids are discovered every year. Robotic telescopes are used to track asteroids that orbit close to us and that could someday collide with Earth.

- Near-Earth asteroids are asteroids that orbit no farther than 121 million miles (195 million km) from the Sun.

- Meteoroids are small, broken-up bits of asteroids (or comets) in space. When they fall through the atmosphere they're called meteors, or shooting stars. Meteorites are the rocky remains of meteors found on Earth.

- The fastest-orbiting object in the solar system is

asteroid 2004 JG6. It goes around the Sun in just 184 days.

- The famous astronomer William Herschel was the first to call these small celestial bodies asteroids in 1802. Asteroid means "starlike" in Greek.

ASTEROID EXPLORATION TIME LINE

1801 Giuseppe Piazzi is the first to discover an asteroid, which is named Ceres

1802 Astronomer Heinrich Olbers discovers asteroid Pallas

1807 Heinrich Olbers discovers Vesta

1884 Astronomer Johann Palisa discovers Ida

1885 Johann Palisa discovers Mathilde

1898 Astronomer Gustav Witt discovers Eros

1906 Astronomer Max Wolf discovers Achilles

1916 Astronomer Grigoriy Neujmin discovers Gaspra

1991 NASA's *Galileo* is the first spacecraft to fly by an asteroid; it takes close-up images of Gaspra

1994 *Galileo* discovers the first satellite (Dactyl) of an asteroid (Ida)

NASA lunar orbiter *Clementine* fails in its flyby mission to Geographos because of a computer problem

1997 NASA's *Near Earth Asteroid Rendezvous* (*NEAR*) space probe flies by Mathilde

1997 *Hubble Space Telescope* studies Vesta

1999 NASA's *Deep Space 1* (*DS1*) probe flies by asteroid Braille

2000 *NEAR* orbiter begins its yearlong orbit of Eros

2001 *NEAR* probe becomes the first spacecraft to land on an asteroid (Eros)

2002 NASA probe *Stardust* makes a flyby of asteroid Annefrank

2005 Japanese sample-return probe *Hayabusa* arrives at Itokawa and collects pieces of the asteroid. Upon its scheduled return to Earth in 2010 it will become the first asteroid sample-return spacecraft (www.jaxa.jp/projects/sat/muses_c/index_e.html)

2011 NASA orbiter *Dawn*, launched in 2007, to arrive at Vesta before beginning its Ceres orbit in 2015 (http://dawn.jpl.nasa.gov)

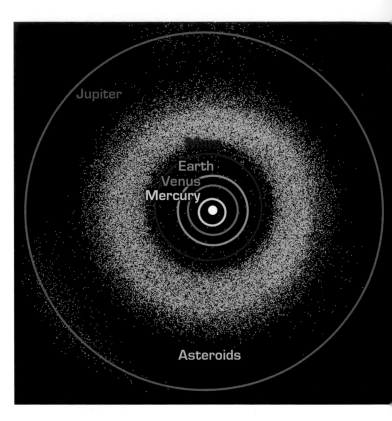

The asteroid belt is between Mars and Jupiter.

Glossary

asteroid a rocky space object from a few hundred feet to several hundred kilometers in diameter

asteroid belt the region of space between the orbits of Mars and Jupiter where most asteroids are found

astronaut a person who travels to space

astronomer a scientist who studies moons, stars, planets, and other space objects

astrophysics a kind of astronomy that studies the physical and chemical properties of space objects

atmosphere the layers of gases that surround a star, planet, moon, or other space object

atmospheric probe a package of instruments that travels through the atmosphere of a planet or moon to study it

ballistic missile a missile that flies under its own power and that is guided in the first part of its flight but that falls freely as it approaches its target

basalt dark gray to black volcanic rock that's usually fine grained

big bang theory the scientific theory that the universe began and expanded after a powerful explosion of a small amount of extremely dense matter

binary code a digital coding system that uses only two symbols, 0 and 1

charged particles electrons, protons, and ions

Cold War the hostile, but not violent, struggle over political differences between the United States and the Soviet Union from about 1946 to 1989

coma a hazy cloud that surrounds the nucleus of a comet

compound telescope a telescope that uses both reflecting mirrors and refracting lenses

comet a space object made of dust, frozen water, and gases that orbits the Sun

concave hollowed or rounded inward like the inside of a bowl

convex curved or rounded outward like the outside of a ball

Copernican system Copernicus's theory that the planets move in circular orbits around the Sun

corona the very hot outer layer of a star's atmosphere

cosmonaut an astronaut from the Soviet Union or Russia

cosmos the universe

density the mass-per-unit volume of something

dwarf planet a round space object that orbits the Sun and may orbit with other objects

eclipse the total or partial shadowing of one space object by another

electromagnetic radiation electromagnetic energy such as gamma rays, x-rays, ultraviolet light, visible light, infrared radiation, microwaves, and radio waves

elliptical shaped like an elongated closed curve, or oval-shaped

escape velocity the minimum velocity, or speed, necessary for an object to escape the gravitational pull of a planet or moon

eyepiece lens the lens of a telescope that is nearest the eye of the observer

flyby probe a space probe that flies by a planet or moon

gamma ray shortwave electromagnetic radiation of very high frequency

gas giant large gaseous and liquid planets with no land (Jupiter, Saturn, Uranus, and Neptune)

gravity the force of attraction between two objects

gravity assist a maneuver or trajectory in which a spacecraft closely passes by a planet or other space object in order to gain momentum from its gravitational field

greenhouse effect the warming effect of a planet's atmosphere

heliocentric having the Sun at the center

hydrazine an ammonia-based liquid used especially in fuels for rocket engines

impact craters craters made by an asteroid, meteorite, or comet

inertia a property of matter by which it remains at rest or in unchanging motion unless acted on by some external force

infrared light invisible electromagnetic radiation that has a long wavelength and that is experienced as heat

inner planets the four planets (Mercury, Venus, Earth, and Mars) between the Sun and the asteroid belt

ion propulsion technology that uses ionized gas to propel a craft

ion an electrically charged particle

Kuiper belt band of billions of chunks and spheres of ice and rock out past Neptune

lander a space probe that sets down on a planet's or moon's surface

launch vehicle a rocket or other vehicle used to get a spacecraft to space

light-year a unit of length in astronomy equal to the distance that light travels in one year, about 5.88 trillion miles (9.46 trillion km)

magnetic field the region of space near an electrically charged planet or moon where the planet's or moon's magnetic forces can be detected

maria the large dark plains on the Moon (also called seas)

mass the amount of matter in an object

matter any kind of substance that takes up space

meteor meteoroids burning up in the atmosphere of a planet or moon; shooting or falling star

meteorite a rock that fell from space

meteoroid a small chunk of space rock, often from a crushed asteroid or a broken-up comet

microgravity near-weightlessness created by free fall or space flight

microwave electromagnetic radiation, characterized by a long wavelength, that can be used to study the universe, communicate with orbiting satellites, and cook

moon a natural satellite orbiting a planet or other space object

moonlet a small moon or natural satellite that orbits a planet or other space object

multi-stage rocket a rocket with smaller rockets stacked on top of larger ones to increase the craft's overall lifting ability

NASA the National Aeronautics and Space Administration; the U.S. space agency

nebula a cloud of gas and dust in space where stars are born

nuclear fission the breaking apart of an atom's nucleus, which usually releases great amounts of energy

nuclear power power that is obtained from nuclear fission and converted into electricity

objective lens the lens of a telescope that is nearest the object being observed

occultation the temporary disappearance from sight of a space object when another object moves between it and the observer

Oort cloud a huge cloud that surrounds our outer solar system and that is home to many comets

orbit a specific path followed by a planet, satellite, or other space object caused by the gravity of the space object it's traveling around

orbiter a space probe that orbits a planet, moon, or other space object

outer planets the planets beyond the asteroid belt

oxidizer a substance that supplies oxygen

parallax the angle between two imaginary lines from two different observation points; can be used to estimate distance

payload cargo carried by a spacecraft

physics the science of matter, energy, and interactions between the two

planet a round space object that orbits the Sun and is alone in its orbit

plasma very hot gases that are good conductors of electricity and that are affected by a magnetic field

primary mirror the main light-gathering surface of a reflective telescope

prism a clear, solid object with flat faces used to separate white light into rainbow colors

probe see *space probe*

propellant the combined fuel and oxidizer that is used by a rocket engine

Ptolemaic system the ancient Greek astronomer Ptolemy's theory that Earth is at the center of the universe

radar a device that sends out radio waves and picks them up again after they strike something and bounce back

radio astronomy the detection and study of radio waves from space

radio waves the type of electromagnetic radiation that has the lowest frequency and the longest wavelength; it is produced by charged particles moving back and forth

Red Planet Mars

reflecting telescope a telescope that focuses incoming light on a mirror

refracting telescope a telescope that focuses incoming light through a lens

regolith loose soil or dust that covers solid rock

retrograde moving in a backward direction

revolution the circling of a smaller space object around a larger one; orbit

rocket a long, narrow, jet-propelled device or vehicle

rocket engine an engine that produces great amounts of thrust by burning both fuel and oxygen and shooting the resulting hot gases through a nozzle

rotation the spin of a space object

rover a vehicle or robot that is used to explore the surface of another planet or other space object

sample-return probe a space probe that collects rock, soil, dust, or gases from a planet or other space object and delivers the sample or samples back to Earth

satellite an object that orbits around a larger space object; a moon; an artificial satellite, like a weather satellite or the *Hubble Space Telescope*

soft land (v) to land without damaging the spacecraft

solar flare a magnetic storm on the Sun's surface, which shows up as a sudden increase in brightness

solar wind a continuous stream of charged particles released from the Sun outward into space

Soviet Union see USSR

space probe unmanned spacecraft launched into space to collect information about the solar system

spectroscope an instrument that separates light and other electromagnetic radiation into their various wavelengths

spectroscopy the study of spectra to determine the chemical composition and physical properties of substances

spectrum a band of colors that forms when visible light passes through a prism

star a space object, made of hot gases, that radiates energy

starscape the background pattern of stars seen in the night sky

sunspot a magnetic storm on the Sun's surface that shows up as a dark area

synchronous rotation the phenomenon in which a satellite's rotation, or spin, time is equal to its orbit time

tectonic activity the movement and shifting of a planet's surface because of changes in the material underneath its surface

terrestrial planet rocky, solid planet with a metal core (Mercury, Venus, Earth, and Mars)

thrust the forward or upward force of a spacecraft or rocket

trajectory the path a space object or spacecraft follows through space

transit the passage of a smaller space object across the disk of a larger one

ultraviolet ray invisible electromagnetic radiation that has a very short wavelength

universe all of space, in which everything in existence is contained

USSR Union of Soviet Socialist Republics, or the Soviet Union, a federation of communist states in Russia, eastern Europe, and northern and central Asia that existed from 1922 to 1991

V-2 the first military rocket, also known as the Vergeltungwaffe 2 (Vengeance Weapon 2)

vacuum space that is empty of matter

visible light electromagnetic radiation that human eyes can see

weight the force exerted on mass by gravity

x-ray penetrating electromagnetic radiation with an extremely short wavelength

Resources

Web Sites to Explore

(Look for specific space mission Web sites on the exploration time lines in the Field Guide.)

SOLAR SYSTEM EXPLORATION SITES

*Imagine the Universe
http://imagine.gsfc.nasa.gov
Older kids (14 and up) will enjoy this site, which was created by the Laboratory for High Energy Astrophysics. It's full of the latest news about space travel and the universe, detailed resources, and activities.

Lunar and Planetary Science at the National Space Science Data Center (NSSDC)
http://nssdc.gsfc.nasa.gov/planetary/
The NSSDC resources available on this Web site include planetary fact sheets, a chronology of lunar and planetary exploration, online books, image resources, and information about individual space missions.

The Eight Planets
www.eightplanets.org
This site gives an overview of the history, mythology, and up-to-date scientific facts of each of the planets and moons in our solar system. Each page provides information and images, as well as references for further reading.

Russian Space Web
www.russianspaceweb.com
News on current Russian space missions and a comprehensive history of Soviet space endeavors can be found here.

Solar System Exploration
http://solarsystem.nasa.gov
This NASA site has nearly everything you'd ever want to know about the solar system, from the latest news and mission profiles to planetary facts for kids. Click on "History" to reach an interactive time line of robotic space probes.

Space.com
www.space.com
Here you'll find space news galore, plus background information on missions and the science and technology behind them.

*The Space Place
http://spaceplace.nasa.gov
NASA's Web site for kids features all kinds of information, games, projects, and fun activities.

*Starchild
http://starchild.gsfc.nasa.gov
This Learning Center for Young Astronomers Web site features information on the solar system, universe, and space science at two reading levels.

Views of the Solar System
www.solarviews.com
This multimedia Web site presents information about the Sun, planets, moons, comets, and asteroids, as well as information on the history of space exploration, rocketry, early astronauts, and space missions.

*Windows to the Universe
www.windows.ucar.edu
A comprehensive site about the Earth and space science that is written at three reading levels from which visitors may choose. The site includes many resources for teachers, too.

NASA FOR EDUCATORS

NASA has a mind-boggling array of resources for teachers and other educators—dive in!

Education Home Page
http://education.nasa.gov

Educational Resources
www.nasa.gov (click on "for Educators")

Educator Links and Lesson Plans
http://quest.nasa.gov

Basics of Space Flight
www2.jpl.nasa.gov/basics
This online spaceflight training module was created by the Jet Propulsion Laboratory (JPL) to help its employees and contractors understand everything that's involved in deep space missions. The site is also popular with high school and college students as well as with space buffs of all ages.

SPACE AGENCY HOME PAGES

National Aeronautics and Space Administration
www.nasa.gov

Canadian Space Agency
www.space.gc.ca

China National Space Administration
www.cnsa.gov.cn (click on "English")

European Space Agency
www.esa.int

French Space Agency
www.cnes.fr (click on "English")

Italian Space Agency
www.asi.it (click on "English")

Japanese Aerospace Exploration Agency
www.jaxa.jp (click on "English")

Russian Space Agency
www.roscosmos.ru (click on UK flag icon)

SKY CALENDAR SITES

These sites will help you find what you're looking for in the night sky—from moon phases to upcoming meteor showers to the current positions of the planets.

http://heavens-above.com

www.space.com/spacewatch/sky_calendar.html

http://spaceflight1.nasa.gov/realdata/sightings

http://stardate.org/nightsky/almanac

SPACECRAFT MODEL SITES

Here are some links to spacecraft-model activities, patterns, and instructions. Have at it!

*Balloon-Powered Nanorover Model
http://spaceplace.jpl.nasa.gov/en/kids/muses1.shtml

*_Cassini_ Spacecraft Models
http://saturn.jpl.nasa.gov/kids/activities-model-simple.cfm

*_Hubble Space Telescope_ Model
http://hubblesite.org/the_telescope/hand_held_hubble/

NASA Models Galore
www.nasa.gov/audience/foreducators/topnav/subjects/technology/Models.html

*Paper Models and More
http://solarsystem.nasa.gov/kids/papermodels.cfm

*These Web sites are appropriate for young people.

Books to Read

Beatty, J. Kelly, et al. _The New Solar System_. Cambridge, MA: Cambridge University Press, 1999.

*Bredeson, Carmen. _NASA Planetary Spacecraft_. Berkeley Heights, NJ: Enslow Publishers, 2000.

Herrmann, Dieter B. _The History of Astronomy from Herschel to Hertzsprung_. Cambridge, MA: Cambridge University Press, 1984.

Kraemer, Robert S. _Beyond the Moon: A Golden Age of Planetary Exploration 1971–1978_. Washington, D.C., Smithsonian Institution Press, 2000.

*Lauber, Patricia. _Journey to the Planets_. New York: Crown Publishers, 1993.

Morrison, David. _Exploring Planetary Worlds_. New York: Scientific American Library, 1993.

Neal, Valerie. _Spaceflight: A Smithsonian Guide_. New York: Macmillan, 1995.

Panek, Richard. _Seeing and Believing: How the Telescope Opened Our Eyes and Minds to the Heavens_. New York: Viking, 1998.

Pannekoek, Anton. _A History of Astronomy_. Mineola, NY: Dover Publications, 1989.

Schorn, Ronald A. _Planetary Astronomy: From Ancient Times to the Third Millennium_. College Station, TX: Texas A&M University Press, 1998.

Sheehan, William. _Worlds in the Sky_. Tucson, AZ: University of Arizona Press, 1992.

Siddiqi, Asif A. _Deep Space Chronicle: A Chronology of Deep Space and Planetary Probes, 1958–2000_. Washington, D.C.: NASA, 2002.

*Spangenburg, R., and Diane Moser. _Exploring the Reaches of the Solar System_. New York: Facts on File, 1990.

*Spangenburg, R., and Diane Moser. _Opening the Space Frontier_. New York: Facts on File, 1989.

*Vogt, Gregory L. _The Solar System: Facts and Exploration_. New York, NY: Twenty-First Century Books, 1995.

* These books were written for young people.

Index